THE ENVY
OF
The World

Other Books by Ellis Cose

The Press
A Nation of Strangers
The Rage of a Privileged Class
A Man's World
Color-Blind
The Best Defense

THE ENVY
OF
The World

ON BEING A BLACK MAN IN AMERICA

ELLIS COSE

WASHINGTON SQUARE PRESS
PUBLISHED BY POCKET BOOKS
New York London Toronto Sydney Singapore

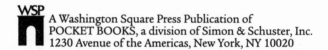
A Washington Square Press Publication of
POCKET BOOKS, a division of Simon & Schuster, Inc.
1230 Avenue of the Americas, New York, NY 10020

Copyright © 2002 by Ellis Cose

ISBN: 0-7434-2715-7

First Washington Square Press hardcover printing January 2002

10   9   8   7   6   5   4   3   2   1

WASHINGTON SQUARE PRESS and colophon are
registered trademarks of Simon & Schuster, Inc.

For information regarding special discounts for bulk purchases,
please contact Simon & Schuster Special Sales at 1-800-456-6798
or business@simonandschuster.com

Printed in the U.S.A.

For Bobby Austin, who as founder and leader of the Village Foundation has devoted himself to serving those men and boys society is most likely to forget. And for my brothers, Robert and Larry, and my friends Oliver and John, who all, in their very different ways, refuse to live the stereotype.

Acknowledgments

No book blossoms without a champion. Tracy Sherrod, a dynamic black woman and my editor, is this book's resident guardian angel. She deserves much of the credit (or condemnation, if you choose) for what I have wrought.

Michael Congdon, my longtime agent and friend, has (as usual) provided invaluable counsel and guidance during every phase of this project. I remain heavily in his debt.

Bobby Austin and Paul Brock provided not only wise advice but also a pipeline to people around the country who helped to shape my thinking as this book progressed from conception to completion.

Lee, my wife—partner, critic, muse—read and worried over every word, struggled with me over every chapter, and contributed more than she could know.

Mark Whitaker, Jon Meacham, and Tom Watson, my editors at *Newsweek,* gave both support and friendship, without which this book could not have been written.

I owe most of all to the scores of men, black and Latino, who shared their hopes, thoughts, and experiences. They provided not only the soul of this book but the reason for writing it. I salute and thank them.

As is the tradition, I accept all responsibilities for the work's shortcomings—for those shortcomings, at any rate, for whom I can find no one else to blame.

I mean, I don't know what the fuss is about. I mean, everything in the world loves you. White men love you. They spend so much time worrying about your penis they forget their own. . . . And white women? They chase you all to every corner of the earth, feel for you under every bed. . . . Colored women worry themselves into bad health just trying to hang on to your cuffs. Even little children—white and black, boys and girls—spend all their childhood eating their hearts out 'cause they think you don't love them. And if that ain't enough, you love yourselves. Nothing in the world loves a black man more than another black man. . . . It looks to me like you the envy of the world.

—from *Sula,*
a novel by Toni Morrison

Contents

A Group Apart

I'm not exactly sure when I realized that black males are special, that the world sets us apart from normal humanity, that we evoke, in not quite equal measure, inescapable feelings of envy and loathing. It dawned, I'm sure, like most great truths—in barely perceptible stages, tangled up inextricably in the mundane puzzles and preoccupations of life.

I do recall some of the childhood incidents that awakened me to that truth, incidents that, sometimes in painful ways, spelled out the difference between black and white. One began on a pleasant enough note. I had gone to Marshall Field and Company, a large department store in Chicago, to buy my mother a gift. As I roamed through the impressive emporium, assessing what my few dollars could buy in such an expensive and intimidating place, I realized that I was being followed—and that my stalker was a member of the store's security force.

From one section of Marshall Field's to another, the guard shadowed me, his surveillance conspicuous and obnoxious. Determined not to be cowed, I continued to browse, trying as best I could to ignore the man who was practically walking in lockstep with me. Finally, unable to contain myself, I whirled to face him. I shouted something—I no longer remember what—a yelp of wounded pride and outrage. Instead of responding, the man stood his ground, staring at me with an expression that combined amusement and disdain.

We must have glared at each other for several seconds, as the realization slowly seeped into my brain that I was no more a match for him and his contempt than a mouse was for a cat. I shuffled out, conceding him the victory, my previously sunny mood eclipsed by barely controlled anger.

Decades after that day, I remember my emotions precisely—the impotent rage, the stinging resentment, the embarrassment, the intense disappointment at myself (for not standing firm in the face of the man's silent bullying, for allowing a bigot to make me feel like a fool, for being unable to crack the guard's smug self-assurance). Yet, as acutely as I recall my feelings, I cannot recollect a single distinctive feature of my tormentor's face. I doubt that it's just the passage of time. On some level, I *wanted* to forget— or at least forget the parts of the experience not useful to remember.

I have written about this incident previously, in *The Rage of a Privileged Class*. I dredge it up again because it was, for me, a defining moment. It was far from the most dramatic encounter of my youth, but it forced me to think deeply, in a way I previously had not, about how easily I could be stripped of my individuality, of my humanity, about how easily racial preconceptions could render irrelevant (at least at first glance) any truth about who I truly was. In the guard's eyes, I evidently was nothing but a thug, and his job was to run me out of the store—to protect Marshall Field and Company, its clients, and its merchandise from this trash who had wandered in from the streets.

Some years later I experienced a similar humiliation. A

maitre d', claiming he recognized me as a troublemaker, refused to seat me, and ordered me out of a San Francisco restaurant. When I declined to leave, he called the cops—who eventually persuaded me to go. The small financial settlement I got after filing suit against the restaurant did nothing to assuage the anger that raged inside me for months after the incident occurred. At the oddest moments, the smirking face of the blond-haired maitre d' would creep into my mind, and I would fume anew over the fact that it took nothing more than the word of an arrogant white man with an inability to distinguish one black face from another to get the cops to literally kick me to the curb.

To be a black male in America is to recognize such treatment as a routine part of life. For, with minor adjustments of fact, the experiences related above are essentially universal among black urban American males. Some 52 percent of all black men (and 25 percent of black women) believe the police have stopped them unfairly, according to a poll taken by the *Washington Post* in 2001. And when you add to that the countless number who have been hassled unjustly by store clerks, bouncers, and other undiscerning gatekeepers, you pretty much have the entire black male population of the United States. For those of us who are the target, a steady diet of society's contempt is not shrugged off so easily. We tend to react in one of two ways: We either embrace the role we are told constantly that we are expected to play, or we reject the script and endeavor to create our own. For those unwilling to push themselves into the realm of self-invention, models of behavior abound.

Why are so many pimps black? Because sex is one area where (whether merited or not) we have been granted dominance, one area (and you can add certain sports to this) where countless white men envy us (or at least the myth of us) and fear we may outshine them. Pimping is easier (psychologically, at least) than proving ourselves—than winning acceptance—in arenas, such as the classroom, where we have been told we do not belong. We can draw comfort from the cold fact that whatever else *they* may think of us, whatever they may make us think of ourselves, they can never take away the awesome power of our physical gifts.

Like most men, I don't particularly mind being thought of as sexual. There are even circumstances in which I don't mind being thought of as a thug. There are times on the street late at night where such a stereotype provides a measure of protective coloration, so to speak. The problem is that the stereotypes carry a set of connotations—self-fulfilling prognoses—not all of which are either flattering or life preserving. And it is *those* connotations that are likely to get you tossed out of restaurants, refused admittance to stores, and pulled over by the police. It is *those* associated expectations that foretell a future circumscribed by the limits of someone else's imagination, those self-fulfilling prophecies that will have you hustling for pennies instead of reaching for greatness.

We can reject those expectations or we can succumb to them; we can follow the path of our presumed destiny or somehow find another route. The wonder is that so many of us refuse to give in, that we summon the strength to resist society's expectations and discover how truly wonderful—and special—we can be.

Being a black man in America has never been easy. It certainly wasn't for our forefathers. Yet at a time when the entire might of a race-demented society conspired to destroy their dignity, millions managed to hold their heads high. They refused to allow their humanity to be stripped away.

Every generation has its demons. Ours tend not to come clothed in white sheets dangling nooses from their arms. Many of our demons reside deep within us, invisible yet powerful, eating away at our confidence and sense of worth. In the worst case, they drive us to destroy ourselves— or our brothers. And even when they don't kill us outright, they place us at a greater risk—of miseducation, imprisonment, and spiritual-emotional devastation—than any large population in America today.

It's not my intention to minimize the very real and formidable challenges that women face—particularly women of color, who make up the fastest growing segment of America's prison population, who suffer the slings and arrows of outrageous fortune much more deeply, very often, than do men. But that is a subject for another day.

So, for those who are black men, for those who care about us, I invite you to contemplate where we are headed and where we should be going. And I also invite you to spend some time appreciating our accomplishments, as well as our potential, and acknowledging all that we have become and overcome.

We strut through the world like some dusky colossus, looming larger than life itself: a nightmare, a fantasy, an American original—feared, emulated, shunned, desired. We are Colin Powell and Willie Horton, Louis Farrakhan and Tiger Woods, Jesse Jackson and O. J. Simpson, the deliverer and the doomed. We are as complicated, as intriguing, as American history, and in many respects, are every bit as confused. Jazz and rap, art forms that we created and in which we excel, define American music, just as basketball and boxing, two activities that we dominate, are the face of American sport. We set the standard for style and make concrete the meaning of cool. White men in boardrooms envy our style and confidence. (Ally McBeal's nerdy law partner isn't the only one carrying around the likes of Barry White in his head.) White kids in the suburbs want to talk like us, want to walk like us, want to dress like us. Some of them, in their pursuit of ghetto chic, are even flashing rapper-wannabe gold teeth. Yet, as much as they want to be *like* us, they have no desire to *be* us. (Well, maybe some of them *do* want to be Tiger—or Michael.) For as special and gifted as we are, we occupy a tenuous place on this earth. And admired as we may be in the abstract or performing on the court or floodlit stage, when we walk the streets at night, we are more likely to inspire anxiety than affection.

Cradled in America's ambivalence, we embody her con-tradictions. We swagger as if we own the universe, yet strug-gle with our own feelings of powerlessness. And we struggle as well with the knowledge (both exhilarating and over-whelming) that we are deemed extraordinarily dangerous—perhaps the most depraved group anywhere—judging from the numbers of us (approaching a million) in prison and in jail; some 11 percent of all black American males in their twenties and early thirties are currently behind bars. But we are also—think Martin Luther King, think Nelson Mandela, or for that matter Bagger Vance of the epony-mous legend or John Coffey of *The Green Mile*—a shining, global symbol of morality and compassion. Some of us—think Cornel West (part preacher, part pundit, part philosopher poet) or Harvard colleague Henry Louis "Skip"

Gates (scholar, multimedia master, and academic impresario)—are reinvigorating the nation's most venerated temples of learning. And those of us who are neither uplifting the world nor wreaking havoc on it can revel in yet another fashionable identity, one recognizable from Newark to New Delhi: the ebony prince of hip-hop, sovereign and creator of the most danceable rhythms on Earth.

So why, given our status as cultural icons and the inarguable reality of our intellectual accomplishments, are so many of us filled with self-loathing? Why are we still debating whether our great democracy is truly capable of appreciating the true range of our talents and the fullness of our potential? For one thing, we are haunted by stereotypes, rooted in history, that give America's admiration a double edge. The very things she admires about us are, in somewhat different form, what she abhors—and always has. John Coffey, the noble, selfless, gentle giant in *The Green Mile*, is merely the most benign manifestation of a superstitious, sentimental, dim-witted creature not quite on the same intellectual plane as normal human beings. The giant's superior morality is not won through conscious and conscientious inner struggle, but granted at birth, like the untainted but also untutored innocence of a child—a man-child who, in this case at least, dotes on his morally deficient superiors. Similarly, our physical prowess and aggressiveness, so admired in sport, becomes something altogether different in noncelebrity mortals, who are less likely to be received with the blissful anticipation accorded a Michael Jordan or a Tiger Woods (who are seen either as "superblacks" or as heroes who have transcended blackness altogether) than with the dread and suspicion that greeted Rodney King—whom the police, in defending their violently aggressive tactics, portrayed as some kind of quasi-mythical beast, imbued with herculean strength and sub-human self-awareness. Even when we are perceived with our morality intact and our brains fully functional, as we drive Miss Daisy or impart mythic wisdom, à la Bagger Vance, we are implicitly advised that our purpose is not to achieve anything for ourselves, but to serve the interests of others, usually white. Such presumptions, although some-what flattering, endow us with characteristics, positive and negative alike, that have less to do with us than with the idea of us, with the dream or nightmare we have come to represent. And *those* are the flattering characterizations. When we are portrayed as less idealized creatures, we can be anything from mack-daddy, jive-talking pimps to soulless, street-smart killers. And unfortunately, being human, many of us take those fanciful, often destructive images to heart and try to fashion an identity out of them. But given such powerful societal preconceptions, how much power do we really have to determine who we are? In today's America that question presents itself from a thousand dif-ferent directions, but let me begin by briefly revisiting the issue of prison.

To put it bluntly, we are watching the largest group of black males in history stumbling through life with a ball and chain wrapped around their legs. The statistics would be shocking were they not so familiar. Some 792,000 black males—a record number—were in U.S. prisons and jails as of June 2000 (more people than live in San Francisco, the twelfth largest city in the United States), a grand metropo-lis of wasted black potential. And there is every sign that things are getting worse. Unless we somehow change our present course, one out of four black boys living in

America today will spend at least part of his life locked down.

How have we reached this sorry point? I'll have much more to say about this later, but allow me to make a few points in passing. Over the last several years, researchers have generated reams of statistics that demonstrate, among other things, that racial prejudice plays a substantial role in who gets arrested, in who gets convicted, in who is written off and hung out to dry. But this vast social tragedy can't all be attributed to a conspiracy of the system. Much of the responsibility lies closer to home. There is something very wrong with the way many of us are defining our place in the world, and that something is landing a lot of us in jail.

Much of it has to do with an attitude all too common in the streets, an attitude that encourages young people, especially young black men, to sabotage their future. It "helps us embrace negativity, embrace sickness. . . . We're proud of having been in juvenile [detention], in the penitentiary. . . . [People] celebrate at funerals . . . with a fifty dollar bag of marijuana. . . . 'Your boy' got killed. You go all out." The observations come from Zachary Donald, a young man who is part of a remarkable group of "street soldiers" who belong to the Omega Boys Club (more on that later) in San Francisco. And the sickness Donald alludes to is not confined to any one urban area.

In Los Angeles, a man in his early twenties a few months out of prison tried to explain to me why he had ended up involved in armed assault, drug dealing, and a long list of other crimes. His mother and father, he explained, were serious, church-going people who cared deeply for him and had tried to instruct him in proper values—as they had tried to instruct his five brothers and three sisters. But despite the love and religious values at home, every boy in his family had gotten in trouble with the law. All had been sent to prison. And so had one of the girls. The call of the streets, particularly for the boys, had been too strong, and the parents' influence had been way too weak. "I started hanging around gangs when I was ten years old. I saw the older guys, and I wanted to be like them," he told me. The story told by his mother was much the same. The closest she could come to explaining why seven of her children had ended up in prison was to attribute it to the neighborhood in which they had been raised, a neighborhood where cops assumed any black boy was a thug, where gang leaders were the most respected males around, where it was a lot easier to "affiliate with the wrong people" than to reject them and the suicidal values they represented. And whereas girls had the option of staying at home with Mom, and thereby avoiding situations likely to end with sirens, guns, and handcuffs, boys had no such option—not if they expected to be treated as men.

To his credit, my young friend was trying to re-create himself. He had become part of a group of ex-cons who leaned on each other for support. And he was working with younger boys, some not yet in their teens, trying to get them to envision a better life. He recalled a kid of twelve he had met recently who was convinced he would go to jail. "By talking to him, I tried to get him to see that it doesn't have to be like that."

Yet I was far from persuaded, sincere as he was, that he truly believed what he was saying. The insightful words that tripped off his tongue so easily seemed not unlike a prayer offered to a god who he was not quite convinced existed. Given his particular experiences—as a low-level drug dealer, gang-banger, and police-certified demon—it would have taken a truly indomitable spirit for him to totally turn his back on the assumptions of his past. Holding faith in beautiful, life-affirming possibilities is always a challenge in neighborhoods whose very existence reflects society's judgment that certain communities (and the people who live within them) are not worth much investment. It's easier to accept the message that life is meant to be short and that the only glory we are likely to get is the glory won by following a code of the streets that elevates us by devaluing our kind.

In a world with values so perverted, it's perhaps to be expected that even suicide—which we once, with some justification, thought of as a white thing—is increasingly becoming a black thing, and more specifically, a young black male thing. From 1980 to 1996 the suicide rate more than doubled among black males from fifteen to nineteen years of age. Obviously, no one explanation could make sense of thousands of unnatural and unnecessary deaths (and here I'm talking not only about those who killed themselves intentionally, but those who died from sticking needles in their veins or from ending up on the unforgiving end of a rival's gun) but allow me a few speculations.

Many of us are lost in this America of the twenty-first century. We are less sure of our place in the world than our predecessors, in part because our options, our potential choices, are so much grander than theirs. So we are trapped in a paradox. We know, whether we admit it openly or not, that in many respects things are better than they have ever been for us. This is a time, after all, when an African American can be secretary of state and, possibly, even president. The old barriers that blocked us at every pass have finally fallen away—or at least they have opened enough to allow a few of us to get through. But although it is fully within our power, collectively and individually, to achieve a level of success that would have been all but unimaginable for most of our forefathers, many of us are doomed to fail.

The deck is stacked against us in childhood, when we are least equipped to know what we are up against, when—in the absence of strong and wise guidance—we often compound the problem of our racial stigmatization by making unfortunate choices about life. Opportunities for deliverance, bountiful though they may be, are not so easy to spot, and by the time many of us learn of their existence, our optimal moment has passed. So we stay stranded on the road to nowhere.

Some of us, of course, get lucky. We somehow get plucked off the road to failure—a path carved by centuries of racism, a road designed especially for us—and placed on a different path. Yet, even those who make it to the privileged class have found that success in this not-yet-quite-integrated America comes with burdens of its own.

"Do I really *want* to be integrated into a burning house?" James Baldwin famously wondered. If, in fact, the house is not exactly burning, the friction within it periodically generates plenty of heat. For acceptance in that house is frequently provisional, and won at the price of sublimating one's true self, of denying pains others have no reason to share, of ignoring slights others are determined not to see.

There is also the matter of a weakening sense of black community. The gap separating those who make it from those who don't has grown wider. And in that wide space, resentments have grown. Worse, in that huge space, that

wasteland between untapped potential and unlimited possibility, a sense of futility has grown as well. There is "no
place to be comfortable at," as one youth who had tried suicide on several different occasions put it.

In *The Fire Next Time*, written nearly forty years ago,
Baldwin observed that white people were "trapped in a history which they cannot understand; and until they understand it, they cannot be released from it. They have had to
believe for many years, and for innumerable reasons, that
black men are inferior to white men." What has become
clear, in retrospect, is that the white man is not the only one
trapped in that history. We are trapped right there with
him. So many of us approach the world feeling that we
don't really belong, that we really are the brutish figures the
world once perceived us to be.

"You can only be destroyed by believing that you really
are what the white world calls a *nigger*," wrote Baldwin.
Today rap stars build multimillion-dollar fortunes by
embracing the identity imposed from without, by relishing
being "niggers," with all that that implies. We wallow in
stereotypes and call the practice "keeping it real." And we
do so totally without irony, without realizing that much of
the so-called reality we cling to (that black men are sex-
obsessed, strutting sticks of macho dynamite, brimming
with street sense, devoid of intellect, driven only by desire)
is nothing but a tragic myth rooted in a time when white
Americans, in order to feel good about themselves, needed
to believe we were something vile, something disgusting,
something inhumanly strange. For how could such a righteous and religious country justify enslaving people unless
they were less than real human beings? In our anger and
confusion, some of us have emulated—*have become*—the

thing whites feared so much, without bothering to figure out that that thing was never really our authentic selves.

That, I suppose, is only natural. At some fundamental level, people tend to believe that they are what their society tells them they are. Our challenge, as black men, as human beings, is to see beyond the assumptions that limit our existence.

The same year (1963) that Baldwin published *The Fire Next Time* Martin Luther King penned his famous *Letter From the Birmingham Jail.*

That letter was King's defiant response to a group of white clergymen who had counseled him to be patient, to keep his protesters and agitators off the street. But justice, King pointed out, was not prepared to wait. And neither was he. "I am in Birmingham because injustice is here," he proclaimed.

To see Birmingham today is to see a very different city than the one where King occupied a place of dubious honor in the local jail. During a visit there, I found myself at a dinner table with the city's mayor, a black man. He and the white constituents with whom he was dining were eager to put the old Birmingham behind them and to celebrate what the new Birmingham had become. No longer a place of oppression, Birmingham is a barometer of progress, a would-be symbol of how things have changed, for whites, for blacks, male and female alike.

The very week—September 2000—that found me in Birmingham also saw James Perkins, a black man, elected to the mayoralty in Selma—the first black man ever elected to the post. And to make things even more symbolically poignant, he was replacing Joe Smitherman, a symbol of the old South, a man so mired in the old way of thinking that he had argued during his campaign that Selma needed a white mayor to keep industry and white residents from fleeing.

That such a blatant appeal to racism did not pay off says something hopeful about the America we are now constructing—though, given that most of the voters were black, Perkin's victory doesn't exactly prove that Alabama has become paradise. Still, how do we square the very obvious progress with the fact that so many of us feel thoroughly incapable of reaping any of its fruits? How do we square the lifting of barriers with the fact that black men are literally falling in droves, destroyed by everything from bullets to depression to AIDS?

We begin by recognizing a simple fact: Though this may be the best time ever to be a black man in America (*and here comes the all-important fine print*), you only prosper if you make it through the gauntlet. And that gauntlet is ringed with bullies armed with ugly half-truths with which they will try their damnedest to beat you to death. So what you must remember is this: Your best chance at life lies in rejecting what they—what much of America—tells you that you are, perhaps rejecting, in the process, ideas you have harbored for most of your existence of what it means to be black and male.

Being a black man in the twenty-first century is a very complicated thing. It requires us to be open to unprecedented possibilities. It also compels us to acknowledge that all the success some of us enjoy is not enough when so many—by some standards, the majority of black men—are denied the opportunity to share it. It requires us to rethink who and what we are and, as we have done so many times in the past, to invent ourselves anew. This book, this extended letter, is not meant as the final word on what that process will entail. The aim is a great deal more modest. It is more in the nature of an invitation to contemplate the possibilities of the journey yet before us, and a review of some of the strategies required to arrive at the end of that journey intact. It is also an acknowledgment of the strength, beauty, pain, and confusion of those of us negotiating our continued survival in a country that still can't decide whether it most wants to love us or lock us down.

1

A Song of Celebration

Let me begin this section with a simple assertion: Black men are not an "endangered species," not in the sense of, say, the peregrine falcon or the bog turtle, whose long-term existences on Earth are in question. We stand nearly seventeen million strong, an ever-growing extended family of black boys and men. We are far too resilient and much too entrenched for the word "endangered" to apply. Precarious as our status may be in many respects (and I will have much more to say about this later), we are not about to disappear. In our centuries-long odyssey as a new race in a New World, we have learned a thing or two about survival, about succeeding against even the longest of odds.

Because the barriers have been so high, we have learned to savor our achievements. We are even learning to appreciate *ourselves*, though the lesson of self-acceptance has not always been an easy one. We are, after all, only a couple of generations removed from the time when black was anything but beautiful; when even our natural physical selves could engender a certain self-loathing—at least among those of us with "nappy" hair and dusky skin.

I recall as a child of perhaps seven or eight coming across some pictures of Africans in a book and noting that they seemed to be significantly darker than almost anyone that I knew. In trying to reason out why that was so, I drew on my rudimentary grasp of evolution. I concluded that here, under the American sky, which was presumably more benign than the African sun, black people, no longer in need of heavy-duty solar protection, were evolving. We were becoming lighter, and in time, I concluded, we probably would become something approximating white. That realization brought a certain amount of comfort. For though my grasp of science clearly was flawed, my sense of the world was pretty much on target. And in that world of the late fifties and early sixties, good hair was straight, light boys were cute, and great wealth (which to a kid in the Chicago housing projects meant such things as a house with a lawn and a bedroom of one's own) was the special preserve of whites. In the universe of wondrous things, as I understood from my time watching television and the occasional movie, blacks were almost as rare as jellyfish in a desert.

That particularly skewed televised view of America began to change during the great civil rights awakening, when black people pointed out the obvious: We were—and always had been—an essential element of the United States, and the wisest and most courageous among us demanded that so-called mainstream America stop pretending that we were interlopers in our own country.

Before the great awakening, before Martin and Malcolm and four little dead girls in a church in Birmingham forced America to glimpse the truth, it was possible to believe that we would stay forever in our slave-society assigned place. Even the geniuses in Hollywood, with all their talent and vision, seemed incapable of conjuring up a world where blacks were equal to whites.

I was reminded of that late one evening when I happened

to catch a broadcast of a science-fiction movie from 1951 entitled *When Worlds Collide*. An errant star (spotted by a brilliant astronomer in South Africa) was hurtling toward Earth, and the best minds of the universe saw no way to stop it. Unwilling to accept mankind's end, which the imminent collision would bring about, the world's scientists searched frantically for a solution. They soon realized that the very instrument of mankind's death, the doomsday star, might be the key to human salvation, that a small planet circling the star seemed capable of supporting human life. The first challenge was to build a spaceship that could reach that star; the second was to choose the forty or so human beings charged with beginning civilization anew.

Those selected were young and suitably beautiful—and every one of them was white. The new Eden, as envisioned by director Rudolph Maté, had no place for blacks (or Asians, or apparently anyone else who would have felt unappreciated in apartheid-era South Africa). I have no idea what concepts informed Maté's racial philosophy, or even whether he consciously had one. I assume that he held no conscious malice toward blacks or any race, but that he was simply oblivious to the possibility that in the new paradise, in a regenerated perfect world, our presence might be desired.

The year of that movie's release also saw the publication of *Invisible Man*, Ralph Ellison's classic journey through American society. I discovered the novel as a teenager, and I was hooked from the opening passage, in which the protagonist declares that he is invisible "simply because people refuse to see me."

The words resonated, not merely because they were written beautifully but because they described so well what I had so often felt. Fact is, they sum up pretty much what virtually any teenage soul perceives. Still, to me it seemed the words were aimed specifically at black boys like me, boys whose value was unrecognized, boys who had to cope with teachers, cops, policemen, and strangers who truly couldn't see us through the stereotypes in their minds, who couldn't imagine a world in which black boys could be as worthy as whites, who saw—to paraphrase Ellison—our surroundings, figments of their imagination, indeed, everything and anything but us.

Thank God that, in the decades since I first picked up that book, attitudes about us have shifted, including, most importantly, our own. Hardly anyone these days doubts that we are an integral part of the human family, hardly anyone disputes the fact that we (some of us, anyway) are awesomely talented souls. But far too often we are still underestimated or told to limit our ambitions, and are forced into that handful of slots where black men are expected to excel. We are athletes, rappers, preachers, singers—and precious little else. Or so is the uninformed assumption, though in truth our talents are as multifarious as our dreams, as uncontainable as rainbow rays shooting across the sky. So let us celebrate all we have done and all that we can be, and let us remember that there always have been black men of sterling character and accomplishment, men as diverse as Frederick Douglass, orator, author, statesmen, and abolitionist, and Dr. Charles Drew, the preeminent blood plasma researcher who organized America and England's plasma programs during World War II. Talented as such men may have been, society embraced them only grudgingly, often not at all, and certainly not in any significant numbers. At long last, that is changing. In an age when black men increasingly are reaching for the stars, and where a couple of us literally have soared into space itself, America finally has begun to acknowledge, and even to rejoice in (albeit selectively), our existence. And the list of achievers is growing apace. It includes men such as Benjamin Carson, a product of Detroit's inner city who became director of pediatric neurosurgery at Johns Hopkins Hospital, and who is renowned, among other things, for separating the Binder Siamese twins in 1987 as the world watched and prayed. And it includes countless others, many less widely acknowledged, who are doing everything from rescuing former gang-bangers from the streets to inspiring young black kids to study science and math.

So let me single out a couple of modern pioneers, not because they are different from the rest of us (in many respects, they are not), but because they are living examples of what we can achieve, with a little luck, ambition, applied intelligence, and sweat.

Maurice Ashley, America's first and so far only black grand master in chess, is a compact man, with a lithe build, glasses, cornrowed hair (at least one afternoon when we talked), and the suggestion of a goatee. He was born in Jamaica in 1966. His parents split up when he was two, and along with his brother and sister, he remained in Jamaica with his grandmother while his mom came to Brooklyn to create a life for them all. She found a clerical job, saved some money, and sent for them when he was twelve.

Ashley had always been an A student and had always been good at games, having learned chess as a child from his older brother. But it was not until he arrived at Brooklyn Technical High School, a highly regarded and selective public school, that he got serious about the game. His interest was fueled in large measure by Chico, a friend from Haiti who dreamed of getting on the school's chess team. But to get on the team, Chico had to rise in the rankings, which he could only do by beating members of the chess club. So he urged Ashley to join the club, with the intention of trouncing him and using his defeat to climb higher on the ladder. Unaware of Chico's motivation, Ashley accepted his invitation. Chico challenged and promptly won, but Ashley didn't much care. By then chess had become his obsession.

He would begin playing around three o'clock, when his classes let out, and stop just before seven, when train passes expired. After doing his homework, he would play chess for another hour and a half. On weekends, he would play all day. Ashley was so involved in chess that his grades began to drop. Instead of As, he got Bs. He was not on the team (good as he was, he was not yet *that* good), but chess had become the center of his life. He loved the competition and felt his game improving, and even dreamed of making a living at it. During his last year of high school, 1983, he boasted to a friend that he would be a grand master within ten years.

He now looks upon that boast as almost comical. "I didn't know what it took to be a grand master, but I had this passion and this love for the game." He also sees clearly, as he did not at the time, just how audacious his ambition was, and how high the odds were against his achieving it. Most grand masters, as Ashley puts it, are "born and bred" to play the game. Much like champion figure skaters who, from the time they can tie on a skate, spend hours a day gliding around the rink, future chess grand masters are molded from the age of five or six, competing in tournaments at a time they barely have learned their ABCs. Ashley was starting awfully late in the game. And he was doing so without the financial and professional support that middle-class white chess whizzes take for granted.

Yet, whereas he could have been pursuing medicine, law, engineering, or any of scores of fields in which blacks had long excelled, he focused only on chess: "I was sort of break-ing the mold . . . this young black kid thinking he's going to be a chess player, putting all of his eggs in this one basket." There was something even mystical in his devotion, a sense that he had a "rope of destiny pulling me along." And since there were no black archetypes at the highest level in orga-nized chess, he went looking for trailblazers elsewhere, for black pioneers who, despite the isolation, had become champions in their sports. Their examples, he figured, would stiffen his own resolution and reassure him that "what I was doing wasn't completely crazy." Debi Thomas, the Olympic medalist and figure skater, along with tennis greats Lori McNeil and Zina Garrison, were among those from whom he drew inspiration. But it was Arthur Ashe who "touched my soul."

It's easy to see why Ashley was so drawn to Ashe, the Wimbledon champ and soft-spoken activist, the thinking man's athlete acutely aware of the racial burdens sitting on his slender shoulders. He was a man who profoundly believed that he had a duty to ignore the limits on aspira-tions imposed on him and other blacks by a society blind to black potential. "My potential is more than can be expressed within the bounds of my race or ethnic identity," wrote Ashe, in his memoir, *Days of Grace*.

People have told Ashley that they see something of Ashe's spirit in him. And it is not a bad spirit for a chess player to have, that of a gentle fighter who never learned to crumble before a challenge. By the time Ashley arrived at

City College of New York (with a short stop en route at New York City Technical College), his hard work and irrepressibly persistent spirit had lifted his level of play. "I had been working at chess consistently—reading, playing, getting into tournaments. My talent merged with my work ethic." He also had discovered, in the Black Bear School of Chess, mentors of his own race in his chosen sport.

The Black Bear School was not a formal institution but a group of men who met in Brooklyn's Prospect Park to play what Ashley calls a ferociously macho, intensely competitive brand of chess. Though the men were not officially ranked, and all worked at other jobs, many played at the master and expert level, and their passion for the game rivaled his own. One of the Black Bears, Willie Johnson, an electrician twenty years Ashley's senior, became something of a mentor and, eventually, godfather to his daughter.

Ashley became captain of the CCNY team and received his master's rating from the United States Chess Federation in 1986. His mother, a single parent who worked as a file clerk at New York University, was proud but less than impressed. "Do you get money with that?" she asked him, her way of pointing out that, although he might be among the top 4 percent of players in the nation, his dreams of greatness and glory through chess were not exactly paying any bills. "You better get a degree, fool," she said.

The baccalaureate in creative writing did not come until seven years later ("That degree was for my mother") but in the interim his chess fantasies blossomed into a career. In the late eighties he began coaching clients for money and, as his reputation spread, he caught the eyes of the American Chess Federation, which provided for him to coach junior high school teams in Harlem and the South Bronx.

The Raging Rooks, the team at Harlem's Adam Clayton Powell Jr. Junior High School that he coached in 1991, was not anyone's idea of a typical chess team. Six out of the eight members had no father in the home. The team captain was living temporarily in a homeless shelter because a junkie had burned down his apartment building. For many of its members, the club was a haven, hollowed ground far removed from the perils and chaos outside. "In that place, nothing brought you down," Ashley recalls. "The attitude was always positive, about success."

Under Ashley's guidance, the Raging Rooks took the 1991 National Junior High School championship, propelling their coach into a media spotlight whose incandescence still astounds him. The *New York Times* ran a front-page feature, and media outlets from across America focused on the miracle worker behind the Harlem chess champs. Among the calls spawned by the extensive publicity came one from Mott Hall Intermediate School in the Harlem–Washington Heights community. "You have to come to my school," said the principal.

Around that time, Ashley had a falling-out with the American Chess Federation. The Harlem Educational Activities Fund, a nonprofit founded by builder Daniel Rose, became Ashley's new angel. With HEAF's backing, Ashely launched a chess program at Mott and repeated the magic, taking their Dark Knights to two Junior Varsity Division championships—in 1994 and 1995. Meanwhile, in 1993, he had ascended to the rank of international master, but despite all his success as a coach, he felt unfulfilled. By 1997, he was fighting depression. "A gaping hole" had opened in his spirit, he confides. "It was the lowest point in my life."

Ashley had proved himself as a coach, and had married and fathered a daughter, but he had not achieved the goal he had set for himself so many years before. It was as if the parade were passing by without him, a feeling that only intensified that April when Tiger Woods, at the age of twenty-one, won the master's by twelve strokes. Woods's feat was unprecedented for anyone, made all the more notable because a person of color, of African ancestry, had achieved it.

Ashley felt more than a twinge of envy. "I said, 'That could be me. I should be making more noise.' " He talked to Courtney Welsh, his supervisor at HEAF, who suggested he talk to the ultimate boss. Daniel Rose granted him a leave with pay and told him to do whatever he needed to do in order to realize his dream.

Ashley hired a coach and launched himself on a routine of international tournaments and concentrated study that culminated in New York in March 1999. In a tournament at the esteemed Manhattan Chess Club International, he racked up enough points to take his seat among the grand masters of the universe. The official title would be conferred that October. The journey that had begun some sixteen years earlier was at long last over.

It was snowing that fourteenth of March, and New York, to the new grand master's eyes, had never looked, well, grander. He was filled with ecstasy and also a bit awestruck at where his audaciousness had taken him, at the fact that a "crazy kid out of Jamaica with a stupid dream" had triumphed in the end. But he did not rest on his laurels for long. Later that year, with HEAF's support, he founded the Harlem Chess Center, a place where neighborhood kids can get instruction, inspiration, and license to keep their dreams alive. "The biggest thing they suffer from is a lack of support," says Ashley. "Like every kid, these kids dream big at first. As you grow, you begin to curb the scope of your dream. You [measure] reality and grow into it."

Despite having achieved his major goal, Ashley continues to aim upward. When I visited him in January 2001, he was ranked seventeenth in the nation. He was hoping to make it into the charmed circle of the top twelve, which would guarantee him a shot at the U.S. championship. He hoped he could do it within a year, but figured that two might be more realistic. And though he has cut back his coaching schedule, the Dark Knights continue to rack up national championships.

That fills Rose with an almost paternal pride. "Our teams, in which there is not a Caucasian face, have the confidence that comes from winning," he boasts. "When our kids are number one in the United States in chess, you don't have to tell them they're good. They know it." Chess, for him, is a means to an end, a way "to tell them they can be just about anything."

Franklin Delano Raines has lived his life proving that lesson. His résumé is a profile in high achievement: graduate of Harvard University and Harvard Law School; Rhodes Scholar; former partner of Lazard Freres & Company, a big-time investment banking firm; former director of the U.S. Office of Management and Budget; and currently head of Fannie Mae, America's third largest corporation—which, in naming Raines chairman and CEO in late 1998, became the first Fortune 500 corporation ever to put a black man in charge.

Not bad for a boy from the poor side of Seattle. But if

Raines's ascendance was not exactly foreordained, he did have greatness thrust upon him, in a sense, virtually at the moment of his birth. Born the fourth of six children in January 1949, his parents named him Franklin Delno—Delno being his father's first name. But "Franklin Delano" was recorded on his birth certificate, making him the namesake of America's revered thirty-second president, a man whose intellect and accomplishments Raines would come to admire. As head of an institution created during Franklin Delano Roosevelt's administration to shore up a housing industry sagging under the weight of the Great Depression (originally an agency of the Federal Housing Administration, Fannie Mae became a private company in 1968), Raines arguably is carrying on the late president's work.

In searching for the secret to Raines's success, many have remarked on the example set by his father, a man who spent five years building, brick by brick, the house that was to be their home. The entire process, recalls Raines, actually took much longer than five years, since the property lay vacant for some time after his dad acquired it, and it took a year and a half just to put in the foundation: "Even when we moved in, it wasn't totally finished." The story finds its way into many of Raines's profiles, as an example of how the father's attributes of persistence and patience naturally took root in the son. Yet, Raines is no patient plodder; he is just the opposite, a man whose impatience is so overpowering that it blew him past the competition with the force of a volcano shooting toward the sky.

His father, who did not graduate from high school, was a mechanic and eventually a parks maintenance supervisor. His mother, who only finished the sixth grade, at one point worked in a chicken house and ended up as a janitor at Boeing. The Rainier Valley neighborhood in which Raines grew up was a mixed-race and working class community on the edge of the central area of Seattle. His neighbors were mostly blacks and Italians, with a few Asians and Jews in the mix. Public housing sat just to the north and the south.

The family consisted not only of Franklin, his parents, and his five siblings, but also a cousin whose mother had died who came to live with them when he was three. Money was never plentiful. For a time the family was on welfare. Franklin himself worked at Irving's Grocery Store, a job he began when he was eight years old. He went to the store every day after school and was there all day Saturday, for which he was paid two dollars a week, a sum that had risen to ten dollars weekly by the time he retired from the grocery business at the age of fourteen.

His family did not especially stress academic achievement: "We went to school because that was what you did." But though his parents were not pushing him toward academic stardom, others were: "Teachers clearly had very high expectations, for me in particular." And among those teachers in his largely nonwhite public grade school (it was roughly 80 percent black, 15 percent Asian American, and 5 percent white, Raines recalls, with the vast majority of the white kids in the neighborhood attending parochial school) black teachers especially pushed Raines to achieve. "You can't screw up," they told him. And he couldn't let them down.

From the beginning, he was grouped with the smart kids, but he noticed, over time, that many of his black peers got weeded out. The fast track, more and more, became the province of Asians, with a few blacks sprinkled in. He is not sure exactly why that happened, but (like Ashley) sees at least part of the phenomenon as a "problem of high expectations." Everyone was expected to do well as children, but as they got older, blacks were expected to do less well.

Nonetheless, he does not remember, as a child, focusing on racial differences. Although it was mostly white kids "constantly coming over to fight us," he saw those skirmishes less as racial conflicts than as public school versus private school fights. He did notice economic disparities: "Some kids had more stuff.... Most kids didn't work. I was working."

In high school, the racial proportions flipped. Approximately 20 percent of the students were black, 15 percent Asian American, and the rest were white. But Raines did not feel intellectually intimidated: "I had grown up competing and playing with white kids." He became state debate champion, quarterback and captain of the football team, and president of the student body.

Franklin High School, as Raines remembers it, was something of a racial "cocoon." To the extent that there was tension, it was generally with "strange whites," people from outside the school who would pick fights with blacks. They were the Washington State equivalent of rednecks, hostile punks spoiling for trouble. "White males to me were dangerous people," says Raines. He vividly recalls a day when a white would-be tough guy approached a well-dressed black man and tried to goad him into battle. Instead of cowing, the black man kicked the bully in the face—a memory (as Raines relives it thirty-plus years later) that fills his voice with awe.

Successful as his high school career turned out to be, Raines occasionally did taste racial frustration. At one point, his debating partner was a white girl. There was no romantic involvement between the two, but the partners sensed resentment. "People didn't approve of a black-white team," says Raines, and that disapproval cost them. Certain debates they clearly should have won were scored in their opponents' favor. He was "pissed," Raines recalls, but far from terminally discouraged. He was headed for a much larger world.

"I never set my sights on Harvard," he says. "Harvard sort of set their sights on me." He came of college age at a time (during the mid sixties) when racial awareness was sweeping the country. The Ivy League suddenly became interested in recruiting a more ethnically and geographically diverse student body. As a champion debater, a star athlete, and a student leader, Raines was a natural target—especially after he took the PSAT (a preliminary college admission exam), on which he remembers doing not spectacularly well, but well enough to keep the Ivy League interested.

At the time, his knowledge of Harvard was, at best, vague. Like so many others outside the elite East Coast orbit, he knew Harvard principally as a name, as a prestigious place where President John F. Kennedy had gone to school. No one in his family had ever gone to college. He didn't even know that many people outside his family who had been to college. Certainly, as a bright and driven kid, he'd assumed he would continue his education *somewhere*, but he had envisioned doing so closer to home, perhaps at the University of Washington or another state college. He had no idea, at the age of sixteen, what going to a place like Harvard could mean, how such a school could fundamentally change the course of his life by providing entrée to a charmed circle of priviledge.

In retrospect, he sees it all clearly. The opportunity to go to Harvard was one—albeit perhaps the most pivotal one—of a series of experiences that would expand Franklin Raines's universe, that would allow him to taste possibilities and to consider options that his parents could only dream of. As a boy of eight or seven, the counselors at the community center where he hung out after school had taken him and several others on trips around and outside the city—to the zoo, the beach, and into a farming area—trips that exposed him to a rich and varied life beyond his neighborhood. (In 1998, during a triumphal homecoming, Raines donated $250,000 to the Atlantic Street Center, citing it as one of the places where "at various parts of my life, people I didn't know lent a hand, and that helped.")

Later, as a debater, he traveled around the state, entering venues he might otherwise never have ventured into. That world was one for which he was sartorially so unprepared that he had to wear hand-me-down sports coats given him by the son of a teacher. The summer between his sophomore and junior years, when he was sixteen, he went to a debate institute at the University of Montana, thanks to a scholarship he obtained through the efforts of his debate coach, Eva Doupe, that enabled him to attend free. (Raines later endowed a public school teaching scholarship in her name at the University of Puget Sound.)

There was other mind-stretching travel as well. Through singing in the school choir, he got to go to Europe, traveling, at the age of seventeen, through Scotland, Wales, England, Germany, France, and Holland—a thirty-day-long voyage of discovery paid for by the choir's fundraising effort. And the following year he went to Washington, D.C., for the first time as a participant in the U.S. Senate Youth Leadership Program, a Hearst Foundation–sponsored project that allowed students to visit historic Washington sites and meet with government officials. He later came to view those years collectively as "a period of time when my world got bigger."

He vividly remembers the morning he first arrived in Massachusetts. He had taken an overnight red-eye flight in order to save money, and eventually found his way to the subway, which he took to Cambridge. He exited at the designated stop and was lost immediately. Where, he wondered, is the university? He was looking for a marker, a conspicuous structure. So he was surprised when an upperclassman pointed out that he was already at Harvard, that Harvard was "all over the place." With the upperclassman's help, he found his residence hall and the three-bedroom suite that would be his new home. His roommates were still asleep. But as he stepped into the suite, weary from his journey, and reflected on the enormity of the move he had made, he experienced, for the first time in his memory, a sharp attack of self-doubt. "Boy, you have really screwed up," he told himself. "You've been able to bluff until now. But here you've gotten beyond your ability."

He recalls the first semester as one of "constant challenges to confidence" during which he was forever meeting people with famous names and otherworldly accomplishments. World champion skaters, published poets, mathematical geniuses, and fifteen-year-old freshmen were practically run-of-the-mill. And when you ran into a Rockefeller at Harvard, learned Raines, he was likely to "really be a Rockefeller." Surrounded by lots of students from fancy prep schools and special accelerated programs, he immediately realized that many had had a huge head start. And despite his own impressive accomplishments, he felt humbled. Then there was the unfamiliar social environment and the elitist mix of students. Even many of the blacks there were from upper-middle-class backgrounds—despite the fact that some seemed to be posing as up-from-the-street revolutionaries.

Confronted with such a new, bewildering reality, Raines saw the options in rather stark terms. One could either jump in and compete or find another arena where the odds seemed better. For someone with his mindset, there was really no choice at all: "I could not go home disgraced." Just as it had been unthinkable for him to disappoint his teachers and neighbors as a boy, it was unthinkable for him to shrink from this new set of challenges.

He was comforted by a lesson from football. Despite his slender build and less than overwhelming stature, he had become a champion by plunging in and doing his best: "As long as you don't drop the ball, I realized, at some point in that game you're going to get a touchdown, because they stop watching the little guy."

That spirit served him well. He graduated from Harvard magna cum laude in 1971, and went on to Oxford University that fall as a Rhodes scholar. After serving briefly as associate director of Seattle's Model Cities program, he picked up his Harvard law degree. Law made sense to him because he always knew he was blessed with the ability to talk, and had vague thoughts about a possible political career, perhaps emulating, in some sense, politicians such as Franklin Roosevelt and John Kennedy whom he had always admired. He had also admired many of those fighting in the trenches for civil rights, people getting their heads bashed in and suffering police dog bites in order to wrest the bigotry from America's soul, but "I was pretty sure I wasn't brave enough to do what they were doing."

After law school, Raines's star ascended and never came down. In fact, his ascent up America's political-corporate hierarchy actually started while he was an undergrad in 1969, with a summer job working for Daniel Patrick Moynihan, one of his Harvard professors who had become President Richard Nixon's urban affairs adviser. Raines returned to the White House as an intern his last year at Harvard.

Throughout his career, Raines has clung to the lesson he learned at Harvard and on the football field: It's infinitely better to plunge ahead and do what is required than it is to question your abilities and be paralyzed by doubt. So after he became the first black director of the Office of Management and Budget in 1996 and President Clinton asked him to balance the federal budget, he "just got into it," not caring that the budget had not been balanced in over a decade and a half. And he, characteristically, ended up meeting his goal.

As for being the "first black" in so many different positions, Raines professes not to feel unduly burdened by the designation: "I never felt it carried a weight. I felt it carried an obligation." Part of that obligation, as he sees it, is to be aware that eyes are on him, that people, particularly black people, are looking to him as an example of what is possible in the world. Blacks, he observed, are "so suspicious of the establishment that, until the establishment demonstrates it will do something, the assumption is that it will not do anything."

He is touched that people have approached him to say they have been inspired by his words, or by his example. ("I had no idea anyone was paying that much attention.") And he now sees it as part of his mission to "give them something they can shoot at," to help other blacks gain the confidence to say "Running a large company is something I can do."

He believes his appointment as head of Fannie Mae (with its nearly four thousand employees) not only set an important example for blacks but for boards of other big companies who might be inclined to—and yet wary of—naming a black to such a position: "Now other boards of directors see it's safe. . . . breakthrough stuff is sort of a signal that it's okay."

I tell the stories of Ashley and Raines not because I expect you to see them as role models—I'm not sure that I much subscribe to the concept, since I believe we must all find our particular paths instead of plunging, willy-nilly, along someone else's course—but because I see them as slayers of stereotypes, as dazzling examples of ambition fulfilled through throwing off the narrow constraints of racial convention. They are, in other words, men—black men—who didn't let the fact of their goals being untraditional stand in the way of their attaining them. They are men who have made their true selves visible, who were not content to remain, like Ellison's invisible man, defined by the inadequate imaginations of others. They are beacons lighting the path to roads not yet taken. And for those of us who doubt our potential power in the world—and over our own lives— they are vibrant reminders of the indomitability of the aroused human spirit, of the boundless energy waiting to be unchained in the hearts, minds, and souls of black folk.

In some sense, of course, the power of black men has always been acknowledged, but in the past, as previously noted, it was of a purely physical kind, like the power of a prize bull or stud. Even when the black-is-beautiful era dawned, much of America was more inclined to celebrate our physical traits, our tawny and ebony beauty, than our artistic and academic accomplishments.

Thankfully, we now live in an era when it is easy to find so much more about us to celebrate. Sure, many of us are physically beautiful. In an era where superstar models like Tyson Beckford set hearts around the globe aflutter, who can deny that? Whatever prejudice still exists in the world, we finally have gotten even whites to agree that blacks can be truly pretty. And certainly, we—some of us, that is—possess more than our share of athletic gifts. From Muhammad Ali to Michael Jordan, from Derek Jeter and Ken Griffey, Jr., to Tiger Woods, the list of exceptional black athletes stretches on, seemingly into infinity. But we should also celebrate the fact that, despite the pressure to fit our aspirations into the conventional rapper-athlete-gangsta mold, we continue to break new ground, to expand our excellence into unexpected areas, to challenge the notion that anyone other than us can define the essence of who we are. In other words, we should celebrate the fact that we are freer than ever to shake off society's invisible chains and go places our parents could not even imagine—if only we can convince ourselves to believe the growing and abundant evidence of our own fully realized potential.

2

Keeping It Real

She had buried her brother only two weeks earlier, a fact I forgot over the course of the evening until the subject came up over dinner. He had died the day the world celebrated Martin Luther King's birth, of an apparent heroin overdose at the age of forty-five. From sniffing glue as a ten-year-old he had moved on to pot and then heroin, all by the time he was fourteen. He had spent his adolescence and the rest of his abbreviated existence in and out of rehab, in and out of trouble, in and out of his sister's life. As she talked about her brother and his catastrophically bad choices, I could not help but contemplate *her* life. Nelly had become a huge success—a graduate of Cornell University and Albert Einstein College of Medicine, a pediatric physician at Montefiore Medical Center in the Bronx, a mother, a wife (her husband is also a doctor)—while Loquillo, as her big brother had come to be called, had fallen into a drug-drenched ditch and never gotten up.

The evening had begun in a spirit of celebration, with a benefit at New York's Apollo Theater. The beneficiary was the Inner City Scholarship Fund, an arm of the Archdiocese of New York that raises money for Catholic schools in poor urban neighborhoods. Those schools, with their largely black and Latino student bodies, have an astounding record of success. Over 90 percent of the students graduate, and almost all go to college. I was at the event principally because of my wife. A product of inner-city Catholic schools, she had served as mistress of ceremonies for a VIP reception. The concert that followed featured young people reciting poetry, playing music, and dancing, and culminated with a performance by Take Six, an all-male, mostly a cappella gospel group that had left the audience standing, clapping, and swaying to the beat.

At dinner, we touched on the brother and moved on, but I couldn't get the conversation out of my mind. So a few days later, I called Nelly and asked her to explain, as best she could, why their lives had diverged so.

She was not exactly sure. Who could be? The very nature of life is to be a mystery. And why one person turns left and another right can be among the deepest mysteries of all, mysteries inextricably linked to whatever it is we are trying to describe when we talk about free will. But she did point to differences in circumstance that provided plenty of food for reflection.

Loquillo had been born in the Dominican Republic of their mother's first husband. Her spouse was a well-to-do man in his forties and she was still in her teens. That marriage did not work out, and when his mother came to New York to start anew, she left her four-year-old son behind.

By the time she sent for him, he was nine and she was remarried with two new children: a boy who was three years old, and Nelly, who was two. Her big brother, she later learned, took his mother's remarriage as a betrayal and the existence of the other children as a sign that he was no longer loved. He felt "a very, very deep sense of rejection," Nelly realized years later as she read the letters Loquillo wrote while in drug rehabilitation. When Loquillo tried to understand why he had started sniffing glue, he placed much of the blame on the new and expanded household he found awaiting him in a strange new world.

There was also another factor, one that, at least in his mind, explained why Nelly had done so well and he had not. She had made it, he insisted, only because she, with her delicate, European features, "looked white," whereas he looked like a light-skinned African American. She could never quite buy the "looking white" explanation, because despite the racial prejudice she assumes that he faced, he also had a considerable share of advantages. His father, for one thing, had money, enough so that, when Loquillo initially got into trouble, he was shipped off to a boarding school in the Dominican Republic; enough so that, when he got bored, he could take trips to the Bahamas and elsewhere. And even later, when, disgusted by his drug use, Loquillo's father disowned him, race seemed not to raise any particular barriers, at least not for the girlfriends, women of all races, who became his major source of support.

Still, it was clear to Nelly, even when she was a very young child, that he was not particularly proud of his life. She recalls episodes when she was nine or ten of being ushered out of the living room when his druggy friends arrived. Resplendent in a dashiki and a huge afro and grooving to the sounds of Santana, he would hang out with his cronies, and he would give himself over to heroin, his most patient and precious love. But even as drugs consumed him, he "took on the burden of protecting me," she recalls. "If I ever see you smoking pot, I will kick your ass," he would tell her. His mantle of protection extended to the illegal social clubs of Harlem, where she would go to dance into the night. He made it known that she was his little sister and was not to be touched: "Nobody dared come anywhere near me."

Indeed, it was not only her brother but other male relatives who shielded her from the streets in a way that rarely happens with boys. They formed a protective cordon around her and kept would-be corrupters at bay: "They were my protectors. Anyone who messed with me had to go through them first."

But much as she loved those male protectors, she knew that her survival depended on escaping their world. She had seen what happened to the kids who went to George Washington High School in her neighborhood. Many of them ended up in trouble, their future snatched away from them before they reached adulthood. One boy she knew had been shot in the back. Countless others had fallen into a deep hole of despair and given up on life. So though she had little real knowledge of a world away from the one she knew, she set her sights on a Catholic school, Aquinas, where a friend went and where she thought she could learn enough to at least become a secretary. She got to go, in large part through an act of fate: Her father died and the social security money became her ticket to Aquinas. Through Aquinas, she discovered a world of unbounded opportunities, and realized that she could be so much more than someone else's assistant. Her experience, nonetheless, left her with a measure of guilt—a survivor's guilt: "I had to cut those people off [the males who had protected her] in order for me to survive, and yet I made it because of them."

The experience also left her with an understanding of the rage felt not only by her brother but by many young black and brown males. "I see it in my patients. . . . And when it gets directed inward, that rage is incapacitating."

Much of what Nelly had to say resonated strongly with what I have heard elsewhere, particularly from black and Latino males struggling against the violently destructive (and self-destructive) winds that America sends our way, struggling against the dark forces of the street, from which Nelly received such loving protection, to which so many of us surrender before we truly know the cost.

To be a black man, especially a young black man, is to risk seduction by the street. It temps us with its soulful song, offering us a place to belong, the only place—or so we are made to believe—that we alone can own. And the allure can be overwhelming. Like a swimmer in the grip of an under-tow, many of us succumb out of a sense of sheer inevitabil-ity. From the moment our brains are capable of cognition, we are primed to embrace our presumed destiny. I'm not talking about a conscious conspiracy. The truth is more mundane and also more insidious. For the conspiracy (if we choose to call it that) is an unwitting one, yet it shapes our psychological environment and affects—at times controls— our perception of reality. Movies, television, and radio bombard us with images of the black male, images—rein-forced with endless repetition—of the black man as a street-wise, trash-talking operator, as the polar opposite of the refined, cerebral white male who, coincidentally, may con-trol the world but lacks our style and soul. And a powerful subculture in our own communities emphatically reaf-firms that perspective, a subculture violently policed by the hip and the ignorant (by which I don't mean stupid, but simply unaware), paying homage to and perpetuating a suf-focatingly narrow view of black masculinity.

It begins when we can least defend against it, at an age

when we are not even aware it is happening: when we are children, babies, trying to act and think like men. Spencer Holland, an educational psychologist, noticed it when working with first-graders in one of the District of Columbia's poorest and most forsaken neighborhoods. The girls were happily singing a song about the ABCs, but the boys were hanging back. The song was "girls' stuff," the boys explained. Holland was astounded at their attitude, at the idea that children so young had already absorbed such "macho images of what a male is and what a female is." With a little coaxing from Holland and his male colleagues, the boys joined in and soon were singing just as enthusiastically as the girls, but the experience caused Holland to reflect deeply on the fact that when it comes to role models in school, boys begin at a disadvantage, that they are surrounded, for the most part, by women, whom they have no interest in emulating, so they pluck notions out of the atmosphere (or, to be more precise, out of their community culture and from the public airwaves) about the right way for boys to behave.

Holland, determined to provide some guidance, founded Project 2000. Its mission is the saving of souls. The 2000 is for the year, now passed, when the first-graders he led through their ABCs would (assuming all went well) graduate from high school. Many of those youngsters dropped out along the way, but a significant number hung in. And Holland, a committed and emotional man, learned many lessons during their journey—among them that it's a lot easier to get boys to sing out the alphabet than it is to rescue them from the streets. As they get older, somewhere around the ninth or tenth grade, the mother's involvement often drops off. The boys are simply too old to keep track of—or so the moms assume. The boys also sometimes come to see their mothers in a new and less idealized light—particularly if the mothers are involved in drugs or casual sex. The boys become angry with their mothers and angry at the state of their home life and seek solace in the street. "Our major competition," says Holland, "is the drug dealers, who go after the brightest boys."

The lure of drug money for young inner-city boys is so strong because it offers such huge rewards to those who otherwise would have very little. As Kevin, a former drug dealer put it, "I came from poverty and I wanted nice things and money and everything. . . . I quit high school and . . . I just got caught up. . . . It was like, 'I'm eighteen. I want my money *now*.' "

"They want the Jordans, the gold chains. They want instant gratification. . . . Most of them don't believe they're going to make it to see twenty-five." So they want to "get theirs now," says J. W. Hughes.

Hughes knows that reality firsthand. Brought up in a South Side Chicago housing project by a single mom, he followed his older brother into the Disciples street gang around of the time of his ninth birthday. "That's the only thing that there was in our neighborhood, pretty much," he explains. By the time he was twelve he had gone from "snatching purses, snatching chains, selling weed" to armed robbery and dealing powder cocaine. Given where he lived and the path taken by his older brother—by then, a veteran gang-banger—it was simply a natural progression. "If you stay in the projects and it's two thousand people, and you don't see anybody going to work, and the only people who have things are the drug dealers, who are you going to want to be like?" he asks. To his credit, Hughes eventually saw another path, but it took a couple of tragedies and the intervention of a caring older man to clarify his vision. The summer of his thirteenth year as J.W. and Lester, his best friend, were en route to "The Taste of Chicago" (the city's annual lakefront restaurant celebration), rival gang members ambushed them and shot Lester dead. "I remember thinking that could have been me," recalled J.W. Motivated by the shooting and by the family's move to a new community on Chicago's north side, J.W. dropped out of the gang-banger lifestyle, but he continued to sell drugs—including rock cocaine, which, by the mid eighties was all the rage.

It was a drug deal that led to his second awakening: A man he thought was a friend saw an easy score and shot him in the head while J.W. was weighing drugs. Miraculously, he survived. "After that, I said, 'I got to get it together. If I plan to be here, I've got to change.'"

Happily for him, he came upon a mentor who ran an organization called BUILD (Broader Urban Involvement and Leadership Development) that attempts to provide focus for the lives of inner-city males. That mentor, Michael Johnson, brought him books to read, encouraged him to finish high school and college, and eventually offered him a job with BUILD, where Hughes now works trying to help young men who are as lost as he once was.

How do you turn young lives around? Hughes shrugged, and after a moment's reflection, replied, "Through love, man. That's the only way." But the street does not make it easy, as Jesse, a former gang-banger who grew up in the midtown area of Los Angeles, deeply understands. Jesse, who is now in his early thirties, has served time for a string of offenses, drug dealing and armed assault among them.

From a very early age, he recalls, he was convinced that "I was either going to jail or dying [young]." He fell in with the Schoolyard Crips gang as a teenager. He blames peer pressure, wanting to be cool like the guys around him, and the need to escape home: "Being young and not knowing too much, you only look at the glitter." The gang embraced him warmly, as it had virtually every male he knew.

In *Monster*, published in 1993, Kody Scott reconstructs his life as a member of the Crips. Scott, who was nicknamed Monster at the age of thirteen for nearly stomping a man he robbed to death, documents in detail the process of breaking away from his mother: "My homeboys became my family—the older ones were father figures. Each time I shot someone, each time I put another gun on the set, each time I successfully recruited a combat soldier, I was congratulated by my older homeboys." Loyalty to the gang became the paramount virtue and work was the province of dim-witted dupes: "You either jacked for money or you sold dope. Working was considered weak."

"Our environments force us to become predators," was the way one former gang member explained to me his decision to follow a similar path. "We didn't have the strong father figures," he added. Another blamed the cops who, he said, convinced black and Latino males that thug life was their only option: "They see that you live in the neighborhood and they automatically believe you're dumb. . . . Around here, getting beat up by a cop is just normal."

With everyone from jaded, corrupt cops to homeboys on the corner telling us that black men are meant to be thugs, it's not exactly surprising that so many of us end up agreeing. For though giving in to the stereotype, giving one's self over to the streets, means choosing an inordinately difficult life—one that all too frequently ends in jail, serious injuries, or early death—it's also to follow the path of least resistance. Or, perhaps more accurately, it is to follow the only path that many young men see as open to them.

In *Home Is a Dirty Street*, Useni Eugene Perkins explores how street culture has taken over the lives of many young, black men. He is a poet, community activist, youth worker, and educational administrator, but I recall him most fondly as one of those essential adults who, as director of the local Boy's Club, provided guidance and an important model of black male achievement while I was growing up in Chicago. For one thing, points out Perkins, the street is the one place young black men can find genuine sympathy "to their plight." And it contains the older men they respect most—the hustlers and drug dealers who seem infinitely more attractive than the social workers and teachers with whom they have little affinity. So instead of focusing on school, young men take their lessons from the "Street Institution":

> The curriculum for this asphalt institution incorporates many of the same courses that are found in the formal school setting. Political science is learned from the unscrupulous exploits of corrupt politicians; history from years of discrimination and economic deprivation; biology from youths smoking marijuana and having sex in dirty alleys; and the physical sciences are taught by learning how to endure elements unfit for human consumption. . . . [The student's] classroom is his total environment, the alleys, pool halls, taverns, tenements, and the streets on

which he lives. By the age of twelve he has usually taken all the required courses, and is prepared to face the challenges which are thrust upon him. His entry into the street culture, as a full-fledged member, is not certified by a diploma but, rather, by his proven ability to operate within the sanctions of his community. Graduation from the Street Institution never comes for most. Instead, the black child spends the major portion of his life repeating the same courses, so that by the time he reaches adulthood it is almost impossible for him to change his orientation to life. . . . The ghetcolony child automatically becomes a ghetcolony man.

Acceptance of Street Institution style and ethics is not limited to those in the so-called ghetcolony. "Even the guys who are middle class are still supposed to be able to 'get down' with certain values of the street," observed Elijah Anderson, a sociologist at the University of Pennsylvania, who has spent years hanging out in the 'hood pursuing his interest in urban ethnography. The result of those street-level assumptions is what Anderson describes as "a kind of confusion" that manifests itself as a war between the values of "decency" and those of the street.

Alden Loury, now a Chicago journalist, was bewildered while attending the University of Illinois a few years ago and seeing many of his black, middle-class friends passing themselves off as street thugs. "Smart guys, really sharp guys, for some reason seemed to be lured to the idea of being a player, a hustler. You had a lot of brothers out there who wanted to be hard, wanted to be gangstas," recalled

Loury. "I thought we came [to college] to get away from this stuff."

But getting away from such values can be extremely difficult when they are promoted so vigorously and when middle-class values, attitudes, and behaviors (at least when exhibited by blacks) are ridiculed and dismissed as inauthentic. That such thinking illustrates nothing so much as ignorance of our history and culture and—if followed to its logical conclusion—leaves us no place that is truly ours other than the gutter, make it no less potent.

Many members of the black middle class have "become shy," have chosen, in essence, to disguise their middle-class identity, largely because "so many bullets were shot at us," observed Useni Eugene Perkins during a conversation in 2001. And some of the bullets (rhetorical, for the most part) were fired for justifiable reasons. "A lot of us were not sincere, were not honest about our motives. A lot of us profited from programs that were in the community." Consequently, many of us became somewhat ashamed of (or at least ambivalent about) being middle class; and, in certain circles, given certain circumstances, we pretend to be something else—affecting the walk, the attitude, the language, the manner that presumably go over better on the street.

But middle-class guilt is not the entire explanation for the elevation of street values above those of "decency." Many of us simply have come to believe that blacks are not meant to follow conventional patterns of success. We have internalized the message passed along, often subtly, in the attitudes of so many of those who touch our lives.

Stephanie Bell-Rose, a lawyer and foundation executive, has watched the dynamic at work with her two teenage sons. Residents of an upscale suburban community, they are as far removed from the ghetto streets as Beverly Hills is from Appalachia. Still, they are often treated as if they just swaggered in from the state penitentiary.

They go into the same stores as their white friends, but—unlike their friends—they are told to leave if they do not make a purchase immediately. And more than once as they romped around their own community, whites, apparently spooked by their appearance, threatened to call the police. On one occasion, they were skateboarding in a nearly empty school parking lot, where they had gone, at their mother's urging, to avoid the traffic of the street. A woman appeared and, clearly convinced they were up to no good, told them that she would call the cops unless they left the property. Some time later they were feeding ducks at the lake and another woman appeared out of nowhere. She claimed their activities were illegal, threatened to call the police, and pointedly waited for them to leave.

Bell-Rose has spent considerable time "helping them with their reactions" to such events. She has no real worries that her sons will go astray. But she wonders about those who have less support at home, or who have less internal fortitude than her sons. Very often, "black boys begin to live out the perceptions people have of them," she notes. Often those perceptions would be laughable were their collective consequences not so dire.

"I had people come up and ask, 'Are you a Blood or a Crip,' " confided one young man who won a scholarship to a fancy eastern prep school. He left the prep school after one year, largely because of illness in the family, but he made it clear that he was happy to be gone, that the constant pressure of fighting negative preconceptions had taken a heavy toll. The struggle had left him depressed and dispirited, sapping energy he could have devoted more profitably to his studies and his sports. And perhaps more seriously, it had engendered bitterness toward the white world, bitterness that may create problems down the line for himself and those whites with whom he comes into contact.

The alternative to fighting such negative images obviously is to embrace them, even celebrate them, to take this pervasive notion of black masculinity and try our damnedest to be it.

In some respects, it isn't such a bad image. What red-blooded male wouldn't want to be (at times, at least) a cool, swaggering, outlaw sex god who confidently rejects society's conventions? This manufactured black persona obviously appeals to many white teenagers who earnestly attempt to appropriate it—as *Whiteboys*, a 1999 film, comically illustrates.

The movie, directed by Marc Levin, follows the exploits of three white rappers (the "Iowa Gangsta Blood Thugs") determined to be black. "What the hell I want to be white for, man. This shit is stupid," declares Flip, the group's guiding light. Instead, he insists on "keeping it real," which he and his white buddies (who affectionately call each other "nigger") accomplish by assuming thuggish, "black" personas. They dream of going to the big city and doing some "gangster, ghetto . . . project-like shit," which seems to mean becoming big-time drugs dealers en route to transforming themselves into rap stars. Flip prevails upon his one real black acquaintance, a middle-class ex-Chicagoan, to "hook me up with your homies." But the hard-core Chicago ghetto drug dealers he meets through his black friend beat him, take his money, and place Flip in the middle of a shootout, during which a (not altogether innocent) man is killed. Chastened, Flip returns to Iowa, where he presumably reassesses his life. Perhaps most noted for giving the lead female role to Piper Perabo (who went on to greater fame as the star of *Coyote Ugly*—a pseudofeminist, bar-babe fantasy), *Whiteboys* is an intriguing, if exaggerated, portrait of the rebellious white youths known as wiggers (white niggers). It is not the first foray into such territory.

"The White Negro," Norman Mailer's incendiary 1957 essay, exhaustively explored the appeal of a Negro lifestyle to white hipsters. Along the way, Mailer explains why, from his point of view, the American Negro was so uncivilized: "Knowing in the cells of his existence that life was war, nothing but war, the Negro (all exceptions admitted) could rarely afford the sophisticated inhibitions of civilization, and so he kept for his survival the art of the primitive, he lived in the enormous present, he subsisted for his Saturday night kicks, relinquishing the pleasures of the mind for the more obligatory pleasures of the body."

It's easy to understand why educated yet unfulfilled whites might trade a boring existence filled with middle-class responsibilities for a walk through America's cultural wild side, why they might prefer a life with Saturday night kicks and primitive sexual pleasures to one of sensual stagnation. But to define such a lifestyle as black is to reduce black people to the status of unthinking, violent, primal creatures, our animal urges unrestrained by civilization. This characterization, it is worth noting, comes to us courtesy of a self-declared friend, a radical sympathizer to the Negro cause. But it's a double-edged sort of support he offers. For what Mailer and many so-called wiggers are saying is:

Even though black people are simpleminded and uncivilized, we love you anyway, albeit in the way we might love an exotic beast or a crude, untamed wild child. Indeed, we love you more than we love our fellow whites (or at least would prefer to go slumming with you) precisely because you are so crude, because you are so wild and untamed, because you are so clearly keeping it real.

The joke, of course, is on us. For while the white hipsters of the fifties and the wiggers of the present easily can shed their "black" identity whenever they tire of the charade, many of us have taken this hopped-up, thuggish character to be the essence of who and what we are. We even relish in our power as cultural trendsetters, as the ultimate arbiters of cool.

But this power is of a very paradoxical sort. For though we set a substantial part of America's cultural agenda, many of us are living marginal lives and feel incapable of surviving (much less thriving) in the world beyond the 'hood.

In the comedy caper *Double Take*, released in early 2001, a black, Harvard-educated banker on the run from the cops gets this advice from a newfound friend on how to be inconspicuous: "Just act black, that's all you got to do." At another point the would-be buddy accuses the banker of wanting to "be white," apparently because he has a good job and an education, speaks relatively standard English, and chooses not to act like a street-corner pimp. The accuser's idea of what "acting black" entails is clear from his own behavior, which consists of patting a nun on the behind and sprinkling his language with such gems as "Yo bitch, what up?" The Harvard man soon sees the light and becomes a jive-talking boy from the (minstrel) 'hood. In what is apparently meant to be the first-class dining car of a train, he goes into a rant after learning Schlitz malt liquor is not on the menu and loudly accuses the black waiter of "not representing . . . not keeping it real." (How creating a scene in a dinner car serves his objective of appearing inconspicuous is not exactly clear, but then, who ever needed an excuse to make a brother look like a fool.) Any doubt that the Harvard man's essence is truly black vanishes when he demonstrates his hip-hop dance moves in the street.

The movie, obviously, is not to be taken seriously. But it is so evident that it hardly bears pointing out that some of the most serious points are made in jest, or in the name of comedy. When I was child, people would admonish one another affectionately with "Act your age, not your color." And though the comment usually was made in a light-hearted manner, the message is as heavy as an anvil: to act black is to act in a juvenile, irresponsible way—unlike mature, well-mannered whites.

Why are we bombarded constantly with the same hackneyed images of the black man? Why are even many of the so-called positive portrayals (as I suspect those in *Double Take* were intended to be, given that, as becomes clear in the end, the black jive-talkers actually are the good guys) essentially the same—modern variations on what author Donald Bogle (*Toms, Coons, Mulattoes, Mammies & Bucks*) identified as Stepin Fetchit–like "coons" and brutal black "bucks"? The reason is that even in this age of racial enlightenment our idea of race still rests on the shaky foundation of the past.

The black buck goes back at least to *The Birth of a Nation,* D. W. Griffith's 1915 film that presented black men, to use Bogle's language, as "brutes, subhuman and feral . . . big, baadddd niggers, oversexed and savage." No mainstream director working today would dare offer up a vision quite as racist as Griffith's, but modern-day bucks and coons abound in the current cinema. Apparently, inside even the most sophisticated and wealthy black man, there is some dancing creature dying to get out, some uncontrollable force (like the devil inside comedian Flip Wilson) that will cause him to go ghetto.

When Malcolm X talked of even well-educated blacks being niggers, he was making a point about how the white society of that day saw them. He was not suggesting that we turn ourselves into modern-day black bucks. But many of us seem to have confused the message. So in the year 2000 we get the spectacle of Allen Iverson, the Philadelphia 76er and would-be rap artist, insisting on showing how down he can be by rapping, "Man enough to pull a gun, be man enough to squeeze it," only one of the lyrics on his then-unreleased album that provoked a groundswell of protest.

Obviously, most of us who hear such lyric nonsense (and yes, I am well aware that there is good, positive rap music) have the sense to ignore it. We know enough to take such ramblings as nothing more than the posturing of an utterly confused celebrity about what it means to be a man. But it would be naive to believe that such posturing has no real effect. As a reformed armed robber confided, "Any time I went out and robbed anybody, I didn't get into my car and listen to the Isley Brothers. I was going to put on something that was going to pump me up."

Fact is, even without the music my ex-con friend likely

would have done the same thing. It's not as if he tossed his favorite CD into the player and then decided to rob the corner store. The basic decision had been made already; the music simply eased the way—which brings me to this point: Even if the culture of entertainment were not pointing black males toward a life of mayhem and self-destruction, many of us would still feel compelled to live the so-called thug life. Why? Like so much about life as a black male in America, the answer is something of a paradox: Self-destructive as the macho street attitude can be in the long term, in the short term it can be life-preserving, which is to say that the very attitude that sends so many of us to the morgue sometimes can seem like our only hope for survival. And I mean this in both a physical and a psychological sense.

There are, after all, rules to survival in the 'hood. And if you are not prepared to act like "a man," you are presumed to be something less than one; and once that presumption is made, you become fair game. As sociologist Elijah Anderson observes, "Just to be able to face people down . . . to defend yourself [in] compromised environments" sometimes requires a willingness to meet suspicion with violence—or certainly with the threat of violence. And if it takes pulling a trigger to prove we are "man enough" (as Iverson might put it), so be it. In a world where sissies are devoured for sport, a man cannot afford to let his soft side show. It's necessary to get one's "props." Anderson calls it "campaigning for respect," winning a rep that, in effect, envelops one in a kind of protective shield. But that rep can be won only if one is prepared to defend one's honor with one's life, if one is ready to be "a man," in the most distorted sense of the word.

Then there is the matter of inner peace. Everyone, at one

point or another, feels helpless when facing the enormity of life. But for those of us who are black and male, the feeling can be particularly intense. There is so much in our lives that we don't control—from the police who sometimes harass us, to the jobs that so often elude us, to the generally crummy public schools we (or our children) attend—that now and then we go overboard when it comes to our presentation of self—one of the few areas that we do control—and we hide our powerlessness behind a facade of toughness.

We demand respect at virtually any cost, never mind that respect won on the basis of a street rep rarely translates into anything of enduring value, and never mind that whatever protections it may offer on the streets, it increases our odds of ending up behind bars.

Joseph Marshall, Jr., a former schoolteacher in San Francisco, made what was, for me, an arresting observation. "Women are in jail behind love," he said. "Men are in jail because of respect." What he was saying is that by connecting our concept of manhood to a very specific approach to gaining respect, we become coconspirators in our own imprisonment and worse. *Thou shalt not be a punk. Thou shalt not snitch.* "Living by those commandments," Marshall observed, "people end up dead."

Concern about that suicidal approach to life, about self-destructive attitudes pervasive among black men, led Marshall and his colleague Jack Jacqua to found the Omega Boys Club in 1987. Located in the Potrero Hill neighborhood of San Francisco, the club's mission is to rescue lost souls, many of whom do not even know they are lost.

Though a gifted and dedicated teacher, Marshall ultimately found the work frustrating. Many of his students were immensely talented, but talent, he discovered, offered little protection from the perils of the street. One homeless young man, though he was a gifted student, supported himself by working all night selling dope. Others rejected school simply because it did not conform to their idea of cool: "They felt all this pressure from all that they saw. They thought there was something wrong with being good. . . . I learned there were forces operating on these kids that they couldn't get a handle on. For me, that meant I had to go beyond the classroom."

Through group rap sessions and intensive one-on-one work, Marshall tries to show his young associates how to navigate the "maze of life." One incentive he offers is the prospect of a college education, something many had never previously envisioned. As one of his young disciples told me, "We thought college was for Barbie and Biff."

I am both depressed and encouraged by such comments: encouraged because Marshall's outreach works (the young man eventually realized that college is not just for Barbie and Biff), but depressed because it makes absolutely no sense in twenty-first century America for any black man to believe that he is genetically or culturally unsuited for education. Yet many of us still do, even though, in the process, we unwittingly denigrate the memory of our ancestors who were brutalized cruelly—in slave times and afterward—for daring to try to satisfy their thirst for knowledge. Just as many of us continue to equate acting a fool with "acting black."

There is a scene in *Invisible Man* where Ellison's protagonist accidentally bumps into a white stranger, who responds with an epithet. Angered, the black man attacks the stranger violently, demanding an apology. Instead of apologizing, the white man curses him. Moved to rage by the stranger's refusal to acknowledge his demand, the black man beats him brutally and is at the point of slitting his throat but suddenly recovers his senses. Shaken by his own actions, by the fact that he had come to the verge of murdering a fellow human being, the black man stumbles away in horror. The horror soon gives way to humor, as he observes, "Something in this man's thick head had sprung out and beaten him within an inch of his life."

Stereotypes do have a way of taking on a life of their own. And sometimes they beat the life out of people—and not only (or even primarily) out of whites, as is attested to by the fact that black men, murdered at six times the rate of white men, are killed, for the most part, by other black men. Between the ages of eighteen and twenty-four, black men are more than eight times more likely to be convicted of murder than white men in the same age range.

At this point, I have heard all the explanations: poverty, poor schools, low self-esteem, high unemployment, lack of role models, self-hate, misdirected anger at white society, etc. But I doubt that anyone really knows why the disparity is so large, or what particular factors account for what percentage of it. Yet it is clear to me, and I suspect to other thinking people as well (at least to those with the ability to be honest with themselves), that one reason we can be so deadly to each other is that our environment encourages us to be that way. I am speaking not only of the neighborhoods in which we live, where, too often, violence is a way of life, but of the broader cultural environment as well, where racial stereotypes (particularly the one of the brutal black buck) refuse to die.

On a shelf in my office I have a book called *Black & White*

Styles in Conflict, whose author observes, among other things, that blacks' "capacity to deal with intense emotional output is relatively greater than that of whites because blacks have greater experience of being confronted with them." At another point author Thomas Kochman points out that "blacks relinquish to feelings the freedom to exert their *own* will on their behavior."

Even such a revered soul as Toni Morrison can fall back on racial stereotypes. As Bill Clinton endeavored to dig himself out from under the Monica Lewinsky scandal, Morrison came to the somewhat stunning conclusion that Clinton was black. "This is our first black president," she declared in *The New Yorker* in 1998. "Blacker than any actual black person who could ever be elected president in our children's lifetime. After all, Clinton displays almost every trait of blackness—single parent household, born poor, working class, saxophone playing, McDonalds and junk food and fun-lovin' boy from Arkansas."

Perhaps Morrison simply was pulling our collective leg, using literary license to make a political point. But the very idea that there are black traits and white traits, that there is a black way of behaving that is different from the white way of behaving, always seems to leave us on the losing side of the divide.

Why such things as a good education, a good job, and a good command of the English language are still widely considered white is hard to understand, especially since anyone who has watched even a moment of the daytime talk shows should know that whiteness is no guarantee of brains, success, or common sense. Whites who are more moronic and foul-mouthed than even the worst antiblack stereotypes pop up daily on those shows. But despite

Maury, Jerry, and Montel's best efforts to enlighten us, many of us still believe in racial stereotypes that never reflected reality: Whites, genetically and culturally, are academically inclined, and blacks are better at other, less mentally demanding things.

It wouldn't be so bad if when people talked of acting black, they meant acting like a future winner in life—acting like someone who was determined to stay out of jail, get an education, and carve a path through the world that didn't end up on a basketball court or a soundstage. But that, unfortunately, is not the case. So we face this cold reality: For those of us who aren't NBA material, or lucky enough to snare a big time recording contract, practically the only way for us to achieve our dreams (assuming those dreams don't include prison or a dead-end career) is to ignore much of what society tells us (and much of what we tend to tell ourselves) about what it means to be a black male in America. And that is precisely what Mike Gibson has learned to do.

Gibson was a senior at Morehouse College when I talked with him in December 2000. Twenty-five years of age and heavily muscled, he had a cheerful air that belied his long journey through hell. His mother was a drug addict, his father was never around. Mike dropped out of school in the eighth grade and became a petty crook and armed robber who fantasized about his own death. At one point, he confided, he had consumed five hundred dollars worth of crack cocaine at one time, hoping the overdose would kill. On another occasion, he had tried to force himself to slit his own throat. He attributed his death wish to "daily pressure ... post traumatic stress ... seeing people getting murdered, seeing people getting stabbed, a lot of that ... and nobody to talk to." "Who's going to listen?" he asked rhetorically. "The winos in the street?" He also experienced waves of self-pity. "I felt I was the only person in the fuckin' world going through this shit every day."

Mike eventually ended up in juvenile prison, serving a three-year hitch for the attempted murder of a cop. His memories of his time behind bars remain as strong as his resolve to stay on track. From his days in a cell on suicide watch, with a bright light shinning in his face twenty-four hours a day, to his endless time in the hole, prison adds up to an unending nightmare to which he has no intention of returning.

It was during a stretch in the hole that he had his life-changing epiphany. "I left the hole that day feeling like I was tired of being locked up, tired of being in knife fights . . . tired of being incarcerated, of having to watch my back all the time. . . . When I got out, I wanted to do something better with my life."

Nonetheless, immediately after his release, his resolve began to weaken, and there came an evening when he found himself in a car, with a younger brother and a cousin at his side and a shotgun in his hand. Horrified at the road looming ahead, he re-embraced life instead of death. And he made the decision, with Joseph Marshall's backing, to renew his studies and prepare for college. But even then he struggled against the weight of negative expectations, including those from the people to whom he felt closest: "Certain members of my family put me down for going off to college, . . . tried to make me feel guilty for leaving." As a consequence, he was filled with guilt and haunted by doubt: "I went through a period feeling . . . that I didn't deserve to be where I am today."

Mike has learned to squelch that feeling by surrounding himself with "people who want to see me do good," and by reminding himself that false friends have a way of vanishing when times get rough: "When I was in the cell, I was there by myself. . . . I always found myself alone." So he made the decision never to return, a decision he has been able to keep with the help of Marshall and his new homeboys from the Omega Boys Club.

Mike's story, happily, is one of triumph, against an avalanche of unfortunate events and against a river of destructive ideas. In embracing a life-affirming vision of the future, certain family members, old buddies, and old ideas all had to be let go. He, in other words, had to make the choice to leave his old world behind. It is something Spencer Holland, of Project 2000, has seen often with the young men and adolescents with whom he works, men who are trying their best to escape often desperate situations. So he warns them: "As you move up, you will shed some of those who don't have your same goals."

That is not a phenomenon at all peculiar to blacks, or even to the present age. In *Street Corner Society*, published in 1943, sociologist William Foote Whyte wrote: "Both the college boy and the corner boy want to get ahead. The difference between them is that the college boy either does not tie himself to a group of close friends or else is willing to sacrifice his friendship with those who do not advance as fast as he does. The corner boy is tied to his group by a network of reciprocal obligations from which he is either unwilling or unable to break away."

Whyte was not writing about blacks or Latinos, but about Italian Americans living in an East Coast slum he called Cornerville. He wondered why some Italian Americans moved ahead, while others seemed trapped in place. Moving ahead, he concluded, required a choice to leave the old world behind. The Italian-American striver, Whyte noted, "cannot move in both worlds at once; they are so far apart there is hardly any connection between them. If he advances in the first world, he is recognized by society at large as a successful man, but he is recognized in Cornervillle only as an alien to the district. If he advances in the second world, he achieves recognition in Cornerville, but becomes a social outcast to respectable people elsewhere."

More so even than Italians of the 1930s, black men reaching for success in the so-called mainstream world can feel tugged in two directions. On one hand is the pressure to adhere to the code of the streets, to prove that we have not "turned white." On the other are the demands the straight world makes of anyone trying to climb the ladder. At the very least, there is an expectation that differences will be settled with words instead of weapons. While certain "cool" behaviors might be tolerated, even valued, acceptance of street culture goes only so far.

In some respects the worlds may not be quite as far apart as Whyte believed them to be in his day. Basketball players like Iverson, hip-hop entrepreneurs like Sean "Puffy" Combs, and numerous others—particularly in the fields of entertainment and sports—deliberately straddle two worlds, moving back and forth between the corner and the corner suite. In the rap business a street reputation, even if concocted, is all but a de facto prerequisite for success.

During Combs's widely publicized trial for weapons possession, *New Yorker* writer Adam Gopnik made the telling observation about the path to fortune that Puffy had chosen, a path that ran from Westchester to East Hampton, but also crossed through a particular part of Harlem, "a Harlem of the mind and mouth, and you sometimes had to carry a gun to show that you had been there." A Harlem (as Gopnik had no need to spell out explicitly) that is renowned (in certain circles) at the expense of a greater Harlem that has nothing to do with guns and street reps.

Puffy himself acknowledged that his tough-guy street persona was no more than an act. " 'I am definitely the fault of my own image,' " he told the *New York Times* shortly before being exonerated on the weapons charges. "Things like promoting himself as a 'bad guy' and a 'crazy genius.' The 'glitzy, glamorous thing' for which he was famous was just 'rapper-type stuff.' He thought that everyone knew it was a role he played," wrote *Times* reporter Katherine Finkelstein.

Even those who will never be rappers or ballplayers, and who are not chasing dollars through street credibility, though carrying themselves like hard-guy gangstas, often see virtue in staying connected to their old friends in the 'hood.

Damion Samuels, a New Haven native in his late twenties, is proud of the ties he has maintained to the 'hood, despite having gone to the University of Virginia and found a straight job working with youth. Slender, handsome, casually clothed, with long dreadlocks, his look is somewhere between straight and street, and his allegiance is to both worlds.

As a very young man he spent a lot of time hanging out on the streets of New Haven and fell in with a group of people, many of whom were hustling drugs. "Three of my best friends were shot hustling," he recalls. "Two of them had gone to college." One went away to college, but when his money ran out "he fell back on what he knew" and began dealing drugs again. The other went to a school not far from home and consequently never escaped the influence of the old gang. Their involvement in the drug trade led to their being shot. One died and the other was paralyzed.

While in college, whenever Samuels would come home for breaks, he would make a point of hanging out with the old gang. "I felt I couldn't abandon those guys," he said. Recently, an old friend (who was on his way to prison to serve a seven-to-ten-year term) had told him how much those visits had meant, how important it had been to the guys on the corner that Samuels still came back to be with them.

From his own experience, Samuels has realized that one can be in the streets and yet not be consumed by them. And in talking to the young men he counsels at the Harlem Educational Activities Fund, he advises them that they don't have to become total squares to succeed in the world. "I help my young men to understand you can be different ways in different situations, [one way] in college [and another] out with the homeboys."

Such a juggling act, however, requires not only a certain amount of skill, but strength and common sense as well. It requires, among other things, knowing when to tell the homeboys "no," knowing what situations to avoid. And it also helps to have homeboys—as Samuels obviously did— who understand that loyalty has limits; if they insist on going down the road to self-destruction, they shouldn't expect (or demand) allegiance from someone with a different goal in life.

Several years ago I interviewed one of the most impressive teenagers I have had the pleasure of meeting. Antwan Allen, a bespectacled, shy, yet self-assured Harlem resident then sixteen years old, had not had an easy life. His mother, a home attendant and child-care worker, had died from cancer three years earlier, and his father had succumbed to pneumonia shortly thereafter; he had gone to live with an aunt. But thanks largely to the efforts of his mother, he had gotten into a Catholic elementary school, and despite the turmoil caused by her death, he had flourished at a Catholic high school: He became number one in his class, president of the drama club, president of the student council, editor of the school's paper, and head of its honor society. More impressive, he had managed to see through all society's nonsense about "being black."

"Not all black people speak in slang, wear jeans hanging off them, [and are] getting high," he observed. He spoke of a friend who was fighting the pressure to conform to the stereotype of the street. The friend, though bright, was performing far below his ability. Although the friend attended the same school, he was distracted, "so caught up in the whole thing of being 'down,' 'keeping it real,' he's lost all sense of who he is. . . . He slacks off in his work because he doesn't want to be perceived as being white, or being a nerd, or being a geek.' " To Antwan, the friend's behavior was totally illogical. "What is being black?" he asked rhetorically. "I can 'keep it real' on the street corner with my homies, but where is that going to get me in life? . . . I think the only way you can honestly, truly get ahead in life is by staying true to who you are."

Antwan, who went on to study at the University of Pennsylvania, and who was preparing to graduate and thinking of a teaching career when I checked in with him in

2001, was making a very simple point, yet one that too many of us seem to miss: Before we can find our best and essential self, we have to cast off the self imposed on us from without, we have to cast off that brutal thing, to paraphrase Ellison, that sprung from someone else's head. To a greater or lesser extent, we all face that challenge. And we can only triumph if we find the strength to say and make ourselves believe that our worth as men, as black men, has nothing to do (except in a negative sense) with the size of our rep on the street, or even with keeping it real (at least to the extent that real is defined as anything other than being a decent human being). In the end, our worth can only be determined by what we make of who we are, which requires us, for starters, to reject with every fiber of our being the pitiable figure the world would make of us and to discover our own true and better selves, patiently waiting, perhaps unseen, in the outer reaches of our imagination.

3

Too Cool for School

The anger came later—much later, when I was old enough and well traveled enough to realize the extent of the violation, not just of me, but of others stuck in schools not worthy of our trust. At the time I was simply bored. At this point I no longer recall exactly when the boredom hit, whether I was in second or third grade. What I do remember very clearly is the feeling: a sense of frustration culminating in the conclusion that school was a waste of time. It came to me as I was sitting at my desk trying to keep myself interested as the teacher led the class, one listless word at a time, through the book I had read the first day of school, a book (and not a particularly interesting one) she would end up taking the entire semester to slow-walk us through.

What I realized, only in retrospect, was that a crucial set of assumptions had been made, rooted, I presume, in some mixture of experience and preconception. We (poor kids from Chicago's West Side) were deemed essentially unteachable—or at least incapable of keeping up if the teacher proceeded at a normal pace.

Initially, to kill time, I read the dictionary, and when I tired of that, I occupied myself writing and (badly) illustrating comic books, which I peddled to my classmates for their milk money. On a few occasions I sold homework assignments. Once, when a teacher chose a poem I had written as the best in the class, I was surprised, and also taken aback, since I had to sit silent as my friend (to whom I had sold it) smugly took the credit.

That elementary school experience made it difficult for me to take school seriously. I was never a bad student, but I simply didn't see it as a venue where much learning would take place or where my mind would be stretched. And the more schooling I received, the more my assessment was confirmed.

There was the teacher, in either third or fourth grade, who told the class that Negroes had lazy tongues. It was her way, I think, of both challenging and reassuring us, of making us comfortable with our deficiencies in reading and pronunciation (by explaining them as racial traits), while simultaneously suggesting that with will and education we might prevail where others of our race had not. That she herself was black gave the pronouncement a certain credibility. Then there was the seventh-grade teacher who chastised me when I questioned the level of the class reading material. Yes, she agreed, the books were written for fifth graders, but we were not capable of even fifth-grade work, so I had best shut my mouth and be grateful that the school had deigned to give us any books at all.

In many respects, seventh grade was a revelation, for it plunged me into a world where our stupidity was deemed by many of our teachers to be a natural and immutable condition, where the purpose of education therefore was not to enlighten but to help us get through the day. My presence in the class came about as a result of some type of filing error. Instead of tracking me on the basis of my sixth-grade test scores, the school had used my second-grade test scores. Though those were two or three grades above level, they were not where they should have been for one entering the seventh grade. I stumbled upon the error while furtively nosing around in the principal's office one afternoon. Eventually I managed to bring the mistake to someone's attention and to get myself transferred to another class—which, I ultimately discovered, was not much better. But at least in that class they actually tried to teach *something,* instead of simply leaving it to us to amuse ourselves shooting penny pool, shooting craps, practicing kissing technique on willing young women, or otherwise getting into mischief.

Spending several months in what I came to think of as the slow class taught me something about the power of classification and about the tyranny of preconceptions. I learned, among other things, that once a kid is classified as unlikely to learn (barring a very lucky break), he has about as much chance of being reclassified as does a sane man in an insane asylum claiming to have been admitted by mistake. Those months, indeed my entire middle-school experience, also confirmed the lesson I had learned already: School, if taken seriously, could damage both the mind and the soul.

In sharp contrast to my grammar school, my high school was the best public school in the city. Lane Technical High School was then all male and overwhelmingly white and accepted only those who tested at a certain level. But by the time I got there I was so mistrustful of school, so alienated from its methods, and so convinced that I was too smart to be there that I was in no mood to give it my heart. So I made the decision to apply myself only in the courses that interested me. Since the English assignments were boring, I simply refused to do many of them, and though I did very well in math, which I enjoyed (I particularly liked mathematical proofs and the elegant logic they required), I was largely marking time. I never even took the SAT college entrance exam. I was completely oblivious to the world of elite colleges that required the test for admission, and no one bothered to inform me. I instead took the ACT, the exam favored by many schools in the Midwest, and did well enough to get a tuition-paid scholarship at the University of Illinois, which I accepted.

Only years later, during my early twenties, did I realize how unnecessarily inadequate my education experience had been. As a successful journalist traveling around the country, routinely meeting people and colleagues from every sphere of life, it slowly dawned on me that there was a significant difference (and a huge distance) between my own schooling and that of those who were now my professional peers.

Many of my new East Coast friends hailed from some previously unknown world where schools were not just places for hanging out but were stepping-stones in an elaborate grooming process to prepare America's elite. They had done internships at fancy institutions, such as the World Bank and the White House. They had spent their junior years (and sometimes other periods, as well) studying abroad. They had mastered books and areas of learning I had barely sampled. And they knew people of real importance who could open doors to all types of impressive organizations, people whom they had somehow connected with through school.

In glimpsing that world I realized that while I had succeeded in large measure despite school, many of them had succeeded in large measure because of it. And the more I

learned about how they had grown up (with travel, with private tutoring, with expectations of great success), the more
I felt cheated—out of experiences, opportunities, and exposure to options I deserved, or thought I did, no less than
they. And I felt a huge and indiscriminate anger—at my
slum schools and the combination of prejudice and politics
that had created them; at my school counselors, who had
never taught me about this parallel world of learning and
privilege, and at myself, for not having made better use of
my childhood, for not having learned earlier how to gain
access to the advantages my new friends took for granted.
Eventually I was able to place my new insights into some
kind of context and to recognize that in the scheme of
things I was actually very fortunate; for my talent had been
recognized early on, and I had received support as a writer
and would-be independent thinker and scholar that even
many of my socially privileged friends had not.

My experiences, in some respects, are unique. No life,
after all, is precisely the same as any other. But in a general
sense, many of my frustrations, much of my anger, and a
good deal of my naïveté are widely shared, perhaps even, to
some extent, by you. Virtually any bright kid who bumps
up against the typical ghetto school system is bound to be
bruised by the encounter; virtually any black person pursuing an education is bound to run into those who believe
blacks suffer from the intellectual equivalent of lazy
tongues. So I have delved into these personal recollections
to make some broader observations.

Point 1: We often have very good reasons to
believe the educational deck is stacked against
us; because, in fact, it generally is.

Point 2: And therefore our anger and cynicism about the school systems in most of our communities is more than justified.

Point 3: But justified as that bitterness may be, clinging to it will only hurt us in the end.

Spencer Holland, the educational psychologist who runs Washington's Project 2000, told me of a young man he had trained who got the opportunity to go to a school significantly better than the one in his southeast Washington neighborhood. One afternoon he noticed that the youth seemed distressed. Upon talking with him, Holland realized the student was livid—after having learned, in his new and improved school, that the moon's pull on the orbiting Earth was what caused the tides. "Why don't they teach us this in the public school?" the student demanded to know.

On one level the anger seems unreasonable. No school, after all, can teach one everything; and, for most of us, the moon's effect on tides is a rather trivial thing. Yet, for me the story resonated deeply. For it was not so much the one bit of missing information that so bothered the student, but what that missing information symbolized: He had been cheated systematically of knowledge that other kids, no more deserving than he, received as routinely as they receive the oxygen in the air.

Holland has often witnessed the effects of expanding awareness as the world of his students opens up, and he has noted that, along with that awareness often comes anger and sometimes panic: "Anger because they began to understand, fear because they don't know if there's a way out" of the deep hole into which society has plunged them. He routinely warns those going on to largely white institutions to expect to be "envious of all those rich white kids." It is a part of his process of helping to prepare them for engaging the competition in a game rigged against them from birth.

At some point, most of us realize that however rigged the game of learning may be, we have no alternative but to play it. For in today's America, with few exceptions, unless you are talented enough and fortunate enough to get one of a handful of jobs in the sports or entertainment industries, you are lost without a decent education. And the fact that our educational system devalues blacks, particularly blacks who are poor, offers us no exemption from that very harsh reality.

The good news is that today there are some alternatives to wasting time in classrooms where teachers refuse (or don't know how) to teach.

There is the New York–based "Prep for Prep," which identifies "minority group" candidates with high academic and leadership potential and, following some intensive academic preparation, places them in elite prep schools. There is "A Better Chance," based in Boston, which, working with 193 member schools in 27 states, does much the same thing.

If you are a student who has shown academic promise already, such a program literally can save your life; it can pluck you out of a neighborhood infested with gangs, guns, and drugs and leave you ensconced in a fancy private school, where instead of worrying about surviving in the 'hood, you can focus on building a foundation for long-term success. This is not to say that being accepted is to get a ticket to the easy life. The work can be tough, and the adjustment even tougher, as one young man I discussed earlier discovered. It was not just that a white schoolmate asked whether he was a Blood or a Crip, but that the entire atmosphere, as he perceived it, reeked with restrained racism. "You feel like an outcast, not so much because you look different, but [because] the general vibe is not really welcoming. . . . There was a sort of feeling around campus that you're here on a free ride," a sense that "there's no place for you," accompanied by an assumption that black students' abilities were not on a par with whites.

That student met with surprise, even bemusement, when he expressed an interest in sports such as water polo or crew instead of basketball. And there were discussions (such as one justifying slavery) he felt were initiated merely for the purpose of making him feel bad. "It's almost as if they would say things to make a fool of you."

Still, despite all the unpleasantness, he did make some genuine friends, and he also discovered a totally different (and valuable) approach to learning. "They have a much more complex way of examining issues. There are not so many simple yes and no answers."

He seemed unsure whether the benefits were worth the pain, but he could not deny that there had been benefits. For those who stick it out—and many actually enjoy it—the payoff can be huge. The difference in going to a first-rate prep school and attending Typical Ghetto High is the difference between training for a race on a well-balanced diet and training only on soda and cookies: Either way you may make it to the competition, but the odds of winning are just not the same.

A very bright young woman I know had the opportunity to go to a renowned prep school and turned it down. Her mother, who didn't quite understand what was being offered, wanted to keep her daughter close to home. So the daughter went to a mediocre neighborhood school, made it into a mediocre college, and eventually dropped out, unmarried, to have a baby. It's hard to imagine she would be facing the same life options had she taken the scholarship.

The point is that in America (and, in fact, throughout the world), success depends on much more than drive, effort, and ability. Once you achieve a certain minimal competence (and, depending on the field, that level can vary widely), credentials and contacts can count a great deal more than talent. Entry to the schools where the privileged send their own not only ensures access to a superior education but to a world of preferential treatment so blatant, so unrelenting, that it puts affirmative action to shame—a world of credentials and contacts that can put you into games you otherwise might not be aware of, a world of presumed merit that, if you are at all ambitious, you ignore at your peril.

Fancy private high schools, of course, are not for everyone. Daniel Rose, who with his wife, Joanna, founded the Harlem Educational Activities Fund in 1990, takes pride that his program does not skim off the top, that it does not pick only proven achievers from among ambitious inner-city students and transport them to a presumably better, if somewhat alien, world. He believes that any kid of reasonable intelligence, regardless of family background, can become an academic success, given enough guidance, effort, and time, and that it is not necessary to ship young inner-city scholars off to a foreign environment as long as he can transform (or at least enrich) the one in which they already live.

HEAF's offices are located in Harlem, in the former Hotel Theresa, a place that became famous briefly in 1960 when Fidel Castro stayed there. The walls are covered with inspirational paraphernalia, college acceptance letters, pictures, and axioms such as one attributed to George Washington Carver: "Ninety-nine percent of the failures come from people who have the habit of making excuses."

Rose, a middle-aged white man who made his fortune in real estate, presides over HEAF in the manner of a proud grandfather, albeit one who moonlights as a motivational speaker. He strives not only to get across the message that success is possible, but that, for young people from places such as Harlem, it will take a lot of work. "Your chief competitor started yesterday; and you are already a day behind," he is fond of telling his flock. It is his way of telling them that the world's unfairness is not a reason for despair but for redoubling their efforts. "We are preparing our children to compete successfully in a world that is increasingly meritocratic and color neutral," he explains.

HEAF does so by acting as tutor, surrogate parent, and godfather, coaching students for competitive high school and college entry exams, training them in leadership, counseling them on personal problems, even providing blazers for Ivy League university interviews, as well as computers when they go to college, provided that they keep their grades up. No matter how poor the student may be, poverty is never seen as an insurmountable obstacle. "When you are ready for college, the money is ready," says Rose. "No one ever didn't get to the next step because of the money."

In early 2001, Rose counted eighty-plus HEAF participants currently in college (a significant number at some of America's most prestigious institutions) and one hundred-plus in high school. More than 90 percent of those who sign on with HEAF, typically in the seventh grade, stay with it. And the results are clear both in their academic and personal lives. Thus far only two of Rose's children (one a boy and the other a girl) have become teen parents; and they both stayed in school.

Ismael Ovalles, who graduated from Trinity College with HEAF's help, sees the programs as "a supplement to an educational system that is not working at the moment." Born to a teenage mother who never finished high school and a father who was in and out of work but never much of a presence in his life, he found support and stability in HEAF that was lacking elsewhere in his life.

"I was never bad, but I wasn't on the right path," said Ovalles, a twenty-two-year old insurance underwriter. "I've done my share of the street corner." And his school wasn't much good at providing guidance. Even basic things, like providing tutoring or advice on college, seemed beyond the capacity of his neighborhood school, so he got those things from HEAF, which he credits not only with giving him advice but with "changing my perspective" and giving him a broader view of life. Not that he would have been a criminal without HEAF, just that his options would have been reduced sharply. "I might have been satisfied with a substandard life . . . maybe gotten a GED and gone to a city college." As it is, he says, with a touch of wonder in his voice, "I went to a *private* school, nicknamed Little Ivy."

He says it in a way that makes it clear that before HEAF, such an exotic thing as a *private school* had never seemed within the realm of possibility; that, for a poor Dominican kid from his neighborhood, the concept was as foreign as the notion that academics had much of anything to do with real life—as strange as, say, the idea that the moon might have something to do with the tides.

When I reflected on my own anger at my early educational experience, I realized that it was an anger of many facets. There was anger at the poor quality of instruction, at the fact that many of our teachers seemed totally incompetent (or uninterested) in the subject areas they were charged with teaching. There was anger at the low level of expectations that confronted us at every pass, at the assumption, virtually impossible to shake, that we were not deserving of a decent education because we would never amount to anything anyway. And there was particularly strong anger at the fact that we had been kept so much in the dark, that we had never been shown what a proper education could lead to, that we had never been given a real context for the things we were supposedly being taught, never shown how they could connect to a rich and wondrous world beyond our own, that the universe beyond the west side housing projects was, for the most part, as inaccessible as the face of the moon.

Never having been to Washington (or the state capital) and seen government, it was difficult to connect the abstract lessons of political history with anything that might have any connection to real life. Never having been abroad, not even "down south" to Mississippi, it was hard to imagine what purpose geography and foreign languages might have. Never having been to an office other than the one occupied by the principal, it was hard to connect much of anything in school with anything real in the professional world.

This is not to say that sending a schoolchild around the world and showing him fancy offices are essentials of a good education. Many minds have flourished without early exposure to either travel or to the work world. And many with exposure to such things have failed utterly at life. My point is that educators must justify themselves and what they do at least as well as the drug dealer down the street. They must show that school offers something more than simply another way to while away the day—particularly if their students reside in impoverished environments hermetically sealed off from the so-called mainstream. Teachers have a responsibility (whether they seek it or not) to show how education can be a bridge to a new world. But, like so many inner-city schools, mine failed, for the most part, at making us understand their purpose, at showing us any connection between them and the universe beyond. So, when I finally did travel, when I finally did speak another language, when I did spend time in offices where learning translated into money, position, and power, when I saw how the schools other people had gone to had given them a huge head start in life, I felt more than a little resentful. I was upset not only with the schools I had attended (whose responsibility, I knew, was limited) but with the vague entity called society that had created colonies, labeled ghettos, where young boys like myself learned every conceivable lesson in being cool but were kept ignorant of the way the larger world worked and of the skills we would need to survive in it.

Valuable as the academic and emotional support that places like HEAF and Prep for Prep provide may be, their more important function is to release people from the closed "ghetcolony" world, to open minds up to personal possibilities never before imagined—to facilitate the process that Fannie Mae head Franklin Raines referred to as "making one's world bigger."

For someone like Holland, working between the Stanton Elementary School and the Woodland Terrace Housing projects, in one of the most desolate neighborhoods in

Washington, D.C., bearing few resources beyond those he and his team personally can bring to bear, that task can be especially daunting. It is a place in which distractions are easy to come by and the values of education are consistently undermined, a place where, as Holland points out, the most successful men generally have "failed in the educational arena, yet have acquired the 'American Dream' through their involvement in the most negative aspects of the inner-city milieu."

Why did Holland take on such an overwhelming and potentially demoralizing task? In the mid eighties Holland began thinking seriously about "what do we need to do for these little boys?" And the more he thought the angrier he became at the way society treated them. "I was furious . . . and then I got sad. And then I moved past sadness to a place where I could detach emotionally." In that place of detachment he recognized a simple truth, that by imparting a small bit of knowledge, he could create great change. "I can teach anybody to read their ABCs, to count to a hundred. . . . That's what we're not doing in the black community. . . . The overarching problem. . . . *They cannot read.* . . . Look at the people in jail; they read like third- and fourth-graders. I know they're being overwhelmed by other issues as they get older." But without the ability to read and to do simple math by the sixth grade, many young men were lost to society, perhaps forever, he concluded.

Holland throws his whole soul into his work, treating his students as if they were his own children, constantly challenging them to see beyond the present, reaching into his pocket, if necessary, to pay their exam fees and other incidental costs. Nonetheless, he loses a considerable number along the way. One particularly painful loss occurred during the second year of the program, when an eighth-grade boy happened to be in the way when a youth chasing someone else ran into his school firing a gun and unintentionally killed him. Most who fall by the wayside are victims of more mundane forces: They lose interest, move away, or simply get caught up in the culture of the street. In early 2001, of nine boys with whom he had started, three had made it into the current senior class. Of the fifty-five (thirty-four boys and twenty-one girls) that made up the original class projected to graduate from high school in 2000, ten (five boys and five girls) actually stayed with the program and graduated on time. Of those, eight went on to college.

In the white middle-class world, such statistics would be deemed unacceptable, and they are for our community as well, but the harsh truth is that Holland's students, by any measure, are doing significantly better than their peers— peers who are pushed every which way except toward academic success. As one young man told me, "There is a lot of peer pressure to sell dope, to be part of the in crowd, but none to go to school." So we should celebrate Holland's small victories, even as we contemplate why we are losing the larger war. And the reasons are as numerous as the wrongs committed for the sake of race, and all are rooted in the racial assumptions that have haunted us since our arrival in America. These are assumptions that have not only led our country to saddle us with the worse schools in the worse neighborhoods, but also have undermined our confidence to the point that we, in large measure, no longer believe in ourselves—not, at least, when it comes to our ability to do challenging intellectual work.

Zachary Donald, the captain of his high school football team, was outstanding enough as a player to be scouted by several major universities, but, as he now admits eleven years after his high school athletic career, he never thought of himself as college material. Deep down he doubted that he was smart enough to go to a decent college, especially a decent *white* college. When Southern California University came knocking, he dismissed the possibility that such an institution, a college for rich white folks, could be seriously interested in him. "They're not going to accept me in those schools," he thought. And he was so unconnected to college life that the idea he might have a chance at a black school (and football powerhouse) such as Grambling never crossed his mind.

"Go to any high school with black males," he suggested, "and tell them they are smart enough to go to any university in the world. Many of them will say, 'Not me.' I know that because I was one of them." He credits the Omega Boys Club with helping him to see his own potential, as it has helped others who don't see much ability in themselves to see "how wonderful and special [they are]."

I strongly suspect that Donald's insight is correct, that many, perhaps most of us, see serious academics as something beyond us. And a Gallup poll conducted at the end of 1998 only reinforces that supposition.

Bobby Austin, president of the Village Foundation, commissioned the poll, hoping it would facilitate the Alexandra, Virginia–based nonprofit's work of saving young black men. When pollsters probed for an explanation as to why so many black males do less well on standardized tests than most whites, they discovered that nearly 19 percent of blacks (compared to 9 percent of whites) agreed that "African-American males are born with less ability."

That roughly a fifth of blacks profess to believe that black males are innately inferior (at least at learning whatever it is that standardized tests measure) is nothing short of frightening. For what it says is that many of us believe that whatever we do and whatever help we may receive, we are simply genetically not equipped to compete. Given the fact that people characteristically lie, so as to appear more progressive, more open-minded than they actually are, when pollsters ask them about sensitive racial issues, the percentage of blacks who believe we are intellectually inferior is almost certainly higher than 19 percent. (And who knows, if the responses were honest, how high the figure among whites would be!) That means that huge numbers of us lug around a huge burden of self-doubt, one heavy enough to keep us from trying (much less achieving) any measure of scholarly success—though, if we believed in ourselves, we would be as capable of learning as anyone else.

Where do such defeatist attitudes come from? Many of them come from our early exposure to school. As youth worker J. W. Hughes put it: "A lot of our kids don't believe in themselves because they've been told by so many people that they ain't worth shit. . . . I was labeled the bad kid, so I know how that feels." But it's not just teachers who label us; so do movies that instruct us in how to "act black" and newscasters who feed us a steady diet of black criminals but are loathe to showcase black achievers (or even blacks living ordinary middle-class lives). And then there is our entire history on the American continent, a large part of which consists of us being treated as if we were some subcategory of human beings. And though we have resisted such treatment with every fiber of our being, we also have ingested some of the poison in the stereotypes—stereotypes accepted even by some of our white supposed friends.

Let's go back for a second to Norman Mailer's "The White Negro," in which he describes a conversation between a black man and a young white woman with intellectual pretensions. The black man sees through her affectations, not because he is erudite and educated (he can't even read), but because he has some animal-like nose for sniffing out bullshit. Or as Mailer put it, "He had an extraordinary ear and a fine sense of mimicry." So, like some trained monkey, he played back her arguments and then proceeded to deflate them. "Of course the Negro was not learning anything about the merits and demerits of the argument, but he was learning a great deal about a type of girl he had never met before, and that was what he wanted," concluded Mailer.

With a few words, Mailer managed to conjure up roughly half the stereotypes currently in circulation about the black male in America. We are neither intellectually adept, nor particularly curious about ideas, but exceedingly glib, particularly when our target is female, and all the more so when she is white. Although the essay is nearly half a century old, the basic image is easily recognizable today. We see it on the screen, hear it paid homage on CDs, and encounter it daily in the streets in the form of black men and boys who have packaged themselves, albeit unwittingly, in a stylish costume of macho stupidity. When you take the real doubts we harbor about our intellectual abilities and couple them to social alienation, you end up with a prescription not just for thuggish behavior but for large-scale academic disengagement.

Charles Beady, Jr., has been president of Piney Woods, a historically black boarding school outside of Jackson, Mississippi, for some seventeen years, and in those years he has come to expect a certain amount of resistance from many of his male students, people who are, as he puts it, "so bright, so inquisitive, so interesting, so anti-education," people who are so "into being cool" that they feel compelled to hide their intellect, people who also feel the world is stacked against them so there is no point in showing how smart they really are, or in developing their scholastic abilities.

"When I was coming up," notes Beady, who is fifty-three, "There was no way I could aspire to be president. It was just not going to happen. And I think a lot of our youngsters [conclude] that 'something in the environment is going to stop me from realizing my full potential. So why should I act like a fool, knocking my head against the wall?' "

Piney Woods combats students' estrangement through stressing what could best be called old-fashioned values. Founded in 1909 to educate poor blacks in Mississippi, the school remains true to its roots. Nearly half of its three hundred students come from within the state. The rest come from around the nation, a significant number from big cities, sent by parents unwilling to entrust their children to failed inner-city schools. So they have sought out "a safe place," in Beady's words, where their young can get a decent education.

The focus is not only on academics but on manners, chores, discipline, and Christian principles. "We don't have the best academic offerings in the world, but we'll give the kids a good grounding. Some realize they're just as capable as anyone else of high academic achievement," says Beady. With a campus spread across fifty acres in the midst of a two-thousand-acre estate, there is plenty of room for farm animals to roam and plenty of opportunities for city kids to get their hands dirty taking care of livestock.

In his fight against the twin demons of self-doubt and disaffection, Beady has tried everything from counseling and lecturing to recording a CD. *Whatever It Takes (2 Motivate 2-Daze Youth)* is Beady's attempt to connect through the rhythms of hip-hop with a generation of young men who may be way too cool for their own good. "You asked me to keep it real," he raps at one point. "Well, word up dog, this is the deal: Life's a game with rules."

Piney Woods's methods are not guaranteed to turn alienated youths into scholars. About 18 percent of its students leave each year; but of those who stay around and graduate, nearly all go on to college, and a significant number to some of the best schools in the nation.

But even if Piney Woods actually could work miracles, it can only touch the lives of a handful of people. And the same is true of Prep for Prep, HEAF, and the host of other programs and projects working, as Beady puts it, "to ameliorate the sense of futility," to give marginalized people, especially young black males, a shot at an education and a decent life.

Most of us will not be so lucky as to land in some kind of a special program or at an exceptional school especially devoted to our salvation and edification. And even many who do will find it hard to escape the shadow of uncertainty cast by centuries of America's contempt, centuries during which we have been forced constantly to defend ourselves against charges of intellectual inadequacy. That process still goes on today, and it exacts a real cost on our confidence, on our very souls. Many of us, as Beady suggests, simply have given up trying to compete; we have ceded the ground of intellectual ability to whites and Asian Americans. Others of us feel so much pressure to do our best that we end up trying too hard. And we burn out. Or we second-guess ourselves so much that we underperform. We suffer from what psychologist Claude Steele has labeled "stereotype threat."

Interestingly enough, Steele found, the phenomenon is not peculiar to blacks; when white males were told they were competing on tests on which Asians normally did better, the whites went into a slump. "Stereotype threat impaired intellectual functioning in a group unlikely to have any sense of group inferiority," Steele concluded. And among those of us very likely to have a "sense of group inferiority," the consequences can be devastating. We simply self-destruct.

As I write this, documents are strewn across my desk, many attesting to the nature of the current crisis. There is a report released in 2000 by the Village Foundation warning that African-American males are at a higher risk for illiteracy than any group of native-born English speakers. Forty-three percent of black adults (compared to 23 percent of Americans overall) scored at the lowest level of "document literacy," a measure of the ability to understand documents that use both numbers and words. Black males did poorly not only in comparison to white males but to black females. And it is those who can't read, the report notes, who are most likely to end up in either poverty or prison.

I also have in front of me a 1999 report from the College Board, the organization responsible for the SAT (the most widely used college admissions exam), announcing that low expectations and underachievement bedevil us at all levels. "Chronic underachievement among minority students is one of the most crucial problems facing our country today," the president of the College Board observes in a document that points out that not only the poor are affected. Even relatively affluent blacks, Latinos, and Native Americans don't do nearly as well as affluent whites and Asians. In fact, well-to-do blacks do worse, on average, on standardized tests than do the poor whites who take them.

In my files are scores of studies that make the same point: Whatever measure of academic achievement we look at, blacks in general, and black men in particular, aren't doing nearly as well as we should. A large part of the reason, as I have tried to make clear, is that too many of us have simply given up any hope of competing in the academic arena. But another part of the reason, and perhaps, at root, the largest part, is that we are being sabotaged, slowly, gently, sometimes sweetly, but unrelentingly. And the fact that the sabotage, for the most part, is not intentional does not make it one bit less real.

Why do Catholic schools do a good job educating many inner-city youngsters that public schools have failed? For one thing, the students are self-selected and most pay tuition, so they presumably are more motivated to succeed. But there are other important factors as well. Father John Grange, pastor of St. Jerome's, whose Catholic school now serves a predominantly Latino and black population in the Bronx, noted that the difference has little to do with religious beliefs, since the vast majority of those attending St. Jerome's these days are not even Catholic. Nor does it have much to do with resources, since St. Jerome's spends half as much per student as public schools and pays teachers a fraction of the salary and, at the time we talked in early 2001, the school didn't even have a gym. Instead, Father Grange focused on two factors. The first is parental involvement. Parents have to come to at least one big school meeting a year, and they also must come in to pick up their children's report cards. The other (and all important) difference has to with attitude. "We take the kids very seriously. If they do something right, we say that's right. If they do something wrong, we tell them." And instead of expecting children to fail, Catholic schools typically impress upon them the need to achieve, one step at a time. "Kids know they can learn; they have learned; they want to learn," observed Grange. "We insist that we are preparing you for what you're going to do at the next level." In contrast, public schools in poor urban communities are often nothing but factories for failure. Instead of taking black and brown children seriously, instead of treating them as human beings fully capable of great success, they frequently treat them like dullards simply marking time until they are ready to collect welfare or go to prison.

In early 2001 the Civil Rights Project at Harvard reported the results of a series of studies that showed black students were, in effect, screwed from the moment they walked into school. Black students were nearly three times as likely as whites to be labeled "retarded" and twice as likely to be classed as "emotionally disturbed." And black boys were at an exceptionally high risk. Across the board and across the country, blacks were disproportionately tossed into virtually every undesirable mental category school bureaucrats could dream up. Neither poverty nor parental educational attainment explains why so many of our young are being tossed into the educational equivalent of a garbage dump. Blacks (boys, in particular) in more affluent, more racially integrated areas were judged especially at risk—more so than those in ghetto schools, and many times more so than their white classmates—of being designated mentally deficient. But though more likely to be classified as in need of help, nonwhite students were less likely to get it when it could do the most good: "Minority students are less likely than their White counterparts to receive counseling and psychological support when they first exhibit signs of emotional turmoil, and often go without adequate services once identified. This lack of early intervention and support correlates highly with dropouts and expulsion, and helps explain why minority school-aged children are overrepresented in the juvenile justice system." And once packed off to special classes, blacks and Hispanics were significantly less likely than whites to be invited back into normal classes. The ramifications of such widespread misclassification were extremely worrisome, concluded the Civil Rights Project: "To the extent that minority students are misclassified, segregated, or inadequately served, special education can contribute to a denial of equality of opportunity, with devastating results in communities throughout the nation."

The Harvard report is based on just one set of studies, but they fit into a mountain of evidence showing that black and Hispanic children are simply not treated the same as whites. A few years back a nonprofit group in New York decided to investigate reports that black and Latino parents were being discouraged from trying to get their children into classes for the gifted. As I reported in *Color-Blind*:

> Time after time the investigators discovered that black and minority parents were treated differently. The whites were given tours of schools and offered (without prompting) information on programs for the gifted. They were steered away from special education classes or from

schools that employees deemed were not good enough for white children. Blacks and Latinos sometimes found that even getting into the buildings was difficult. And if they did get in, they were generally told only about the "regular" classes.

When I was working on *The Rage of a Privileged Class,* I interviewed scores of college students and graduates, many from exclusive schools, who talked bitterly of the condescension rampant in their universities, of the presumptions of inadequacy they had been forced to overcome, of having teachers, administrators, and fellow students question, generally subtly, whether they were capable of the work the university required. While such patronizing behavior and unintended racial slights were not the defining elements of their college days, many encountered enough of both to mar their entire educational experience.

The accounts rang true not only because so many told stories that were so similar, but because they took me back to a point when I was in my twenties and had decided to study management. At the time, I already had a master's degree in science and public policy and had been an op-ed page columnist and reporter for the Chicago *Sun-Times* for a number of years. I had also worked briefly as an editor and was toying with the idea of a management career. Since I was living in Washington, D.C., and already had one degree from George Washington University, I consulted an administrator in their business school about enrolling in their MBA program. To my astonishment, he immediately launched into a monologue, the essence of which was: Before you can seriously consider getting an MBA here, you first have to make a decent score on the GMAT (a standardized test for business schools). Since I had never seen a standardized test on which I could not do better than 95-plus percent of whites, it had never occurred to me that I might not make GWU's relatively low cutoff score. So as the man rattled on about the test, I found myself getting angrier, until, fed up with his lecture on passing the test and what I considered to be his patronizing attitude, I politely cut him off.

As I walked home and reflected on the conversation, I became angrier by the minute. How dare he assume I couldn't ace that stupid test! How dare he disregard all my accomplishments! How dare he turn a simple request for information into a question about my academic abilities!

Truth is, there may have been absolutely no racial assumptions behind his comments. For all l know, he might have given that same little lecture to a comparable white would-be MBA student. But somehow I doubt it, just as I doubt the validity of the argument, fashionable in conservative circles, that affirmative action created the attitude among certain whites that blacks might not be quite up to speed. I can say, from personal experience, that attitude existed well before affirmative action became such a popular conservative whipping boy.

Some years ago, broadcast journalist Charlie Rose asked me whether I had been discriminated against, whether my race had resulted in my life somehow being worse than it otherwise might have been. I told him that I could not be sure whether my life was worse, only that it was different than it would have been if I had been white. Had I been white, I would not have been born in the neighborhood where I was born, since there were essentially no whites there. I would not have moved to the same public housing project, since Chicago made sure that its projects were segregated. I would not have gone to the elementary schools I had attended, since schools of that sort only existed in the slums. Nor would I have been greeted as much as I had, with the question, generally asked indirectly, "Do you really belong?"

Such a question, of course, does not so much demand an answer as a defense. Unfortunately, the defensive position is one that we—that all of America's suspect groups—so often find ourselves in, defending our right to be something other than we are expected to be, defending, even to ourselves, our right to be whatever we can.

Kirkland Vaughans, a black psychologist friend of mine, thinks schools go a long way toward breaking the spirit of black men. In his interviews with black boys, he has found that even such an apparently benign thing as teaching about slavery—at least the way it tends to be taught in American schools—can drive a stake through the spirit of many young blacks.

"The first point in which we, black people, come into the history books is at the point of slavery. It's as if we did not exist prior to that," Vaughans observed. We are not taught about African civilizations, or about African achievements in science, medicine, politics, and other areas that well predated American civilization; we are taught only about an era in which we were in chains, an era "about which we feel ashamed." Nor are we taught that other groups, including whites, were enslaved. So young people are left with this impression (which is not to be confused with the truth) that of all the groups on the planet, blacks alone were singled out for the degradation and humiliation of slavery, that despite all our wonderful qualities, we were valued most for our muscles and our sweat.

Unable to find a comfortable place in American society, some of us strive to build a civilization of our own. And the world we build, too often, is constructed out of anger, confusion, and pain. Many of the things the straight world—the white world—values, we decide we despise, largely because, as Elijah Anderson puts it, "You don't want to give approval to a society that gives contempt to you."

There is nothing wrong with questioning the values of the white world. There is, after all, much to question: rampant materialism, celebrity worship, limited compassion for peoples considered different. But we tend not so much to question the values as to reject the rules, and to try to replace them with everything from the "code of the streets" to what could be called the "code of self-defeat," where we blow off school and anything that might prepare us for survival in the straight world, but come up with nothing productive to fill the void.

The problem with that approach is that it doesn't exactly remove society's contempt (or the self-doubt, even self-loathing, that society's contempt engenders). It simply makes us contemptuous as well.

Some years ago, when the Reverend Jesse Jackson held his weekly Saturday meetings of Operation PUSH, he often would lead the congregation in a chant.

"I may be black," he would shout.

"But *I am somebody*," the crowd would shout back.

"I may be on welfare."

"But *I am somebody*."

"I may be poor."

"But *I am somebody.*"

On and on, the call and response would go, and at the time I thought it was a bit silly. Of course, we were somebody. Who in their right mind could dispute that?

Yet, over the years, I have realized that lots of people do dispute that, and that a lot of us have a hard time convincing ourselves that we are so much more than society says we are, that we are capable of more than we are assumed to be.

I am not so naive as to believe that we can solve this achievement problem alone, that a simple decision on our part to embrace learning is all that is required. Many of us already have made that decision and find ourselves confounded. Others of us simply have concluded, for very defensible reasons, that there are other things less psychologically fraught that we would rather do with our lives.

Nonetheless, it disturbs me when I hear someone like Beady suggest that many of his brightest students simply don't want to show their intelligence, that that's not considered cool; or when someone like Corey Monroe confides, "We thought college was for Barbie and Biff." Or when a man as bright and motivated as Mike Gibson admits, "Certain members of my family put me down for going off to college."

Too many of us have been taken in by the hype all around us, and perhaps we need to remind ourselves more often that we are more worthy than *they* know, more worthy than we sometimes believe, worthy enough to create a better life than our culture tells us we deserve.

Anger is not necessarily a bad thing, provided it doesn't lead you to sabotage yourself; provided you can use it as a shield against all the negative notions about your ability, against all the voices telling you that you are no one and capable of nothing. Know that you are capable. Know that you can succeed. Know that you are *somebody*. It's not so important that we shout it, but that, deep down, we believe it. In the end, it may be all that saves us from a world that insists we are not.

4

If We Don't Belong in Prison, Why Can't We Stay Out?

A s black men we have endured some of the worst America has to offer—lynchings, enslavement, the indignities of Jim Crow—but never were we coconspirators in our own subjugation—until now. Untold numbers of us stand to lose virtually everything the civil rights struggle won us—the right to vote, to earn a living, to raise our children free from fear—all because we cannot stay out of jail.

"One might have hoped that, by this hour, the very sight of chains on Black flesh, or the very sight of chains, would be so intolerable a sight for the American people, and so unbearable a memory, that they would themselves spontaneously rise up and strike off the manacles," thundered James Baldwin some thirty years ago, as he fumed over the imprisonment of Angela Davis.

Yet here, in this new century, manacles are more fashionable than ever, and they are, in large measure, clamped around the wrists of black men. Nearly a million of us are in prisons or jails. And the Bureau of Justice Statistics (a part of the U.S. Department of Justice) projects that some fourteen million Americans—most of them black and Latino males—will spend some part of their lives locked down. Something obviously has gone horribly awry.

I've never been much for conspiracy theories. I don't believe a group of politicians ever convened and said, "Let's create a system in which twenty-eight percent of all black males—more than one in four of all black boys—eventually will end up in jail." Yet that is the system they created. I don't believe judges and cops plotted to produce a judicial merry-go-around that would shaft black males at every gyration, that would arrest and convict us out of proportion to the crimes we commit and send a disproportionate number of our youths to adult penitentiaries, essentially condemning them to a life without a future. Yet that is what they have produced. Nor do I believe school administrators colluded to capriciously label vast numbers of black boys as "emotionally and behaviorally disturbed," and then conspired to give most of them failing grades, knowing full well that the odds were roughly three to one that once those students dropped out they would end up arrested within five years. Yet again: That is precisely what educational administrators have done.

How did we get to such a screwed-up state? The process began roughly three decades ago with a series of decisions to get "tough on crime," which then, as now, was something of a code phrase with not-so-hidden racial connotations. The get-tough movement was fueled not only by cynical political calculations but by something of a scholarly consensus. During the late sixties and early seventies, some of the most respected scholars in the field of criminal justice concluded that rehabilitation was a sham. An important article by criminologist Robert Martinson, "What Works? Questions and Answers About Prison Reform," essentially said that nothing works. Martinson's article, published in *The Public Interest,* was so influential because, among other things, it reflected the spirit of the time—frustration with coddling wrongdoers, anger at the spiraling crime rate, a new willingness to "lock them up and throw away the key." The same spirit (reinforced by Governor Nelson Rockefeller's personal commitment to stamp out drug use) spawned New York's so-called Rockefeller Drug Laws, harsh measures that mandated stiff sentences for those convicted of holding or selling relatively small amounts of narcotics. Those 1973 laws, in other words, substantially increased prison time for people only marginally involved in drug trafficking. That tough approach set the stage for much of the legislation that was to come, and the disheartening analysis of Martinson and his peers provided the intellectual rationale.

With theories of rehabilitation discredited and public patience exhausted, politicians sensed a huge political payoff in playing hardball with criminals. So prison sentences grew longer, the possibility of parole diminished, and vengeance became an acceptable end in itself. Martinson eventually changed his mind. He published an article repudiating his earlier thesis the year before he committed suicide in 1980. But by then nothing could stop the direction in which criminal justice policy was heading.

So-called truth-in-sentencing laws increased the time most convicts spent behind bars, and tougher drug laws greatly increased the probability of low level drug offenders going to jail. Between 1980 and 1990 the likelihood of people arrested for drug offenses actually getting state prison time more than quintupled. It was a period, not coincidentally, during which a huge private prison industry was born, allowing investors literally to profit from the misery of black and brown men, even as a boom in public prisons allowed the white and rural areas they were generally built in to benefit as well. It was also a time when crack cocaine was flooding into inner-city neighborhoods, setting off alarms across America. Black politicians, fearful the drug would destroy entire communities, demanded that something be done. And white politicians, fearful that drug-crazed thugs would spill out from the ghettos and ignite an orgy of violence elsewhere, were all too happy to oblige. Although blacks were not the major users of cocaine, blacks became the primary law-enforcement target. "Since 1980, no policy has contributed more to the incarceration of African Americans than the 'war on drugs,'" Marc Mauer, a prominent researcher on prison issues, has observed. Meanwhile, Congress increased funding for state prisons and jails and ended prisoner eligibility for the federal tuition assistance offered through the Pell Grant. Never mind that education had proved to be one of the best ways to reduce recidivism. Other amenities also were eliminated or cut back. Why, the politicians asked, should prisoners have weight-lifting equipment, since lifting weights could only make more bulked-up and brutish criminals? And why should they have access to personal clothing, radios, and nonstandard prison food, given that the whole point of prison was to make people suffer? As politicians targeted such so-called frills, they never paused to consider the long-term implications of depriving inmates of the few things that made it possible to maintain a sense of purpose and self-worth.

Indeed, no one in authority seems to have paid much attention at all to the unintended consequences of what

Marc Mauer has labeled the "race to incarcerate." For increasingly large segments of the population, the prison experience became a normal part of life; for young men in certain black and Latino inner-city communities, it practically became an essential rite of passage.

As Jitu Sedike, founder of the Black Awareness Community Development Organization in the Athens Woodcrest area of Los Angeles, observed: "Prison life permeates everything about the community and keeps it down. That's all the young people have to look forward to. . . . Their role models are involved in gang and drug activity. To them, it's a normal process to transition from the streets to prison. It's just as natural as kids in other neighborhoods going from junior high to high school."

A twenty-six-year-old I'll call Frank, who is from the Washington, D.C., area, made much the same point. He went to juvenile penitentiary for the first time at the age of sixteen. His crime was selling drugs, a line of business he took up because "I didn't want to be the only dude on the streets with busted-up shoes, old clothes." He had been in and out of numerous jails and prisons, and when we talked in summer of 2000, he recently had skipped out on probation, vowing, after a quasi-religious experience, never to return to jail. "If I go to jail now," he said, "I know I will die."

He recalled his first trip to the juvenile facility with a certain fondness: "Everybody's like you. It's like a big camp. It wasn't really like punishment." The county jail, where he was sent for selling cocaine at the age of seventeen, was equally agreeable. Initially, he had been worried, fearing that he might be beaten or sexually abused. He discovered, to his delight, that all his buddies were there, so he had what amounted to a fourteen-month vacation before being sent back to the streets. When I asked whether, when he was dealing drugs, he had even been concerned about having a record, he shrugged. "That's all good, because even the girls have been to jail. . . . You go to jail, people want to give you a handshake."

Gerardo Lopez, of Homies Unidos, an outreach program that works with present and former gang members in the Rampart area of Los Angeles (a neighborhood now notorious for the scandal caused by sadistic, crooked cops), believes the movement to put ever younger offenders in prison has had a predictable result. It has practically guaranteed that they will develop into hard-core criminals, for once sucked into the juvenile system, "you have no choice but to blend back into that negative stuff."

A former member of the Savatrucha gang who has spent time in prison himself, Lopez faults the environment in which he grew up, where he now works to stop others from following in his footsteps. "When these guys were in elementary, when they were asked, 'What do you want to be when you grow up?' I'm pretty sure they didn't say 'a criminal.' I'm pretty sure a lot of them said 'baseball players,' 'lawyers,' 'firemen,' or 'good businessman,' or stuff like that," says Lopez. "But it's kind of hard to live up to that dream when you're going to schools here. . . . They stuff about fifty kids into a classroom. The books are all torn up. There're hardly any computers. All the time you're going to school and coming back from school, all you see is drug dealing. You see all kinds of drunk people in the street. . . . You go to school out here, and everybody's mad. Everybody's honking. There're even drive-bys in the morning."

Given the reality of such neighborhoods, prison can seem like a reasonably good alternative, especially when so many people are either headed in or coming out that there is no longer any shame or stigma attached. As one young woman in Philadelphia told me, "One out of every other guy on the block has been to jail in North Philly." In many cases, as "Frank" suggests, prison time is worn like a badge of pride. And even young people who have not been to prison have adopted a prison look.

In a summer 2000 article noting the proliferation of baggy pants, orange jumpsuits, jailhouse denims, white sleeveless T-shirts, bandannas, sneakers without laces, and jeans with one cuff rolled up, *New York Times* reporter Guy Trebay announced the arrival of "incarceration chic." "The jailhouse look is back because it's about rawness, hardness and credibility," one source explained to Trebay.

The phenomenon of jailhouse credibility is not new in black circles. Malcolm X turned his life around in prison. And scores of civil rights leaders, including Dr. Martin Luther King, proudly spent time locked down. Freedom riders and other nonviolent protesters were conscious actors in a political struggle, risking their freedom, and often their lives, for ideals that would make America a better place, that would allow other blacks to live with dignity. Later, when freedom politics took a more radical—and more violent—turn, it was not just jail time, but outright criminality that was celebrated as self-styled revolutionary thugs came to dominate the debate. The most prominent Black Panther leaders were convicted felons, and not just from trumped-up charges resulting from political activism. During his abbreviated life, cofounder Huey Newton undoubtedly did some good work—fighting police brutality and encouraging social and economic development of black communities—but he also was a violent criminal, and was involved in everything from brutal assaults to weapons and drug violations. He was shot to death in 1989, apparently because of his involvement in drugs. Eldridge Cleaver, the party's minister of information, was a rapist. In *Soul On Ice*, Cleaver defended, or at least explained, his rapes as "insurrectionary" acts. He told how he "practiced" on black victims before moving on to more tempting targets: "When I considered myself smooth enough, I crossed the tracks and sought out white prey. I did this consciously, deliberately, willfully, methodically." In his mind, he was not merely committing violent assault but "trampling upon the white man's law, upon his system," while taking revenge for "the historical fact of how the white man had used the black woman."

It was a very small step (really no step at all for the Black Panther party) from defending such demented, depraved criminality to seeing every black inmate, no matter how foul his crime, as a political prisoner, as an innocent victim of a racist America who deserved to be seen as a hero. And with so many white politicians eager to put ever larger numbers of black men into jail, the argument had a certain amount of street credibility.

While the radical rhetoric did not drive the prison buildup (politicians and crack cocaine were more responsible for that), it did make it easier to rationalize in black and revolutionary circles—easier in the sense that going to prison was no longer considered such a bad thing, it was no longer something to be avoided at all costs. It was simply the price to be paid for being a strong black man in America and, therefore, an inescapable part of life.

It seems to me that we are only now beginning to recognize how much damage that attitude (combined with the politically driven "race to incarcerate") has done, not just to those who go to prison, but to their children and to entire communities.

We are creating an entire generation of children whose lives have been deeply marred by prison. At any given time, close to eight hundred thousand black children have at least one parent behind bars, making black children nearly nine times as likely as whites, and Hispanics three times as likely as whites, to have an incarcerated parent.

Teresa Gomez is one person trying to repair the damage to those young souls. A psychologist in her native Peru, Gomez now works as a kindergarten teacher and also runs the after-school program at Abraham House. The South Bronx nonprofit founded by Catholic nuns and priests offers an array of activities and services for prisoners and their families—including tutoring, counseling, and a residential alternative-to-prison program.

Her work with Abraham House has made Gomez an expert in childhood anger, in dealing with the resentment of children as young as five and six who know Daddy can't come home but don't understand why, in coping with their anxiety and bewilderment after being searched before visiting Daddy in prison. "They know [the guard] is not a doctor. They know this is not a school [nurse]. The search can be very traumatic," says Gomez, who constantly wrestles with the question of how to restore the youngsters' self-esteem and motivation and how to shake them out of depression. "Little children don't know how to deal with the situation." So instead of facing their problems, they sometimes pretend that everything is okay, as they try to mask their inner turmoil.

Gomez recognizes the kids have a right to their anger,

that they have a right to be upset because Daddy goes to jail, or because he sits around the house getting high instead of taking care of his family. And she tries to help them not only to work through the anger, but to realize that it's okay to be critical when adults do bad things: "We want them to be critical about not only themselves, but to make their own judgments." Ideally, they will emerge capable of loving Dad but rejecting the behaviors that got Dad in trouble.

That, of course, is asking a lot of young children—especially given how tenuous the ties typically are between inmate and child. Most men are not living with their children at the time they get incarcerated, and, once locked up, most don't see them even once during the period they spend behind bars. Nonetheless, when asked about the importance of their children to them, men in prison invariably say that the children are very important. In a survey conducted among black prisoners in New York State, Garry Mendez, Jr., founder of the National Trust for the Development of African-American Men, found 92 percent saying they wanted better relationships with their kids. And most said they felt guilty about being separated from them.

But, as with so much in life, there is a chasm separating words and actions, between wanting to be connected to children and actually making the connection, between wanting to be a good influence and actually becoming one. For anyone in prison, the process of negotiating the distance between good acts and good intentions is necessarily difficult—and particularly when it comes to children. Indeed, for a parent, the very act of being in prison usually constitutes child abuse. The parent's imprisonment subjects the child not only to separation (and to the loss of family income that may entail) but to a host of other emotional and developmental risks. Despite all the macho posturing that can make serving—and surviving—prison time seem like a worthy accomplishment, very few (if any) small children take pride in having a dad abandon them for jail. They are more likely to feel humiliation as they try to explain to their friends and even to themselves, why Dad is missing, a sense of shame that leads some children to create a fictitious father to replace the one who isn't home. And there is the dampening effect prison can have on young aspirations, for if prison is where Dad is, it doesn't take a large leap of logic for a child to conclude he or she will end up there as well.

One former drug dealer confided that it was thinking of his children, and the example he was setting for them, that caused him to give up his one-time lifestyle: "For me to sell drugs was like me stabbing myself in the throat and my kids watching me do it." But for each inmate so motivated, there seem to be two dozen with excuses as to why they can't change. And it is not only children who are hurt. Anyone close to someone in prison generally ends up carrying part of the emotional and financial burden.

As one ex-wife of a prisoner confided to my *Newsweek* colleague Ana Figueroa:

> When you're involved with someone in prison, that consumes most of your life. You constantly worry about the stuff that happens in there . . . . When I started at UCLA, I lived a secret life. . . . I didn't have anyone to talk to. I couldn't tell people about my husband. . . .
>
> When my husband came out the first time, I had to drop out of school. I was spending so much time trying to research his case and find a

lawyer for him. I had to prepare myself mentally, economically, and legally for him to get out. . . . When a family member comes out of prison, you have to be all things to him. . . . You have to be a psychologist, social worker, and unemployment office rolled into one. Often, the little things that we take for granted are big challenges. My husband was freaked out by things like getting on the bus. . . . People in prison, especially in high security, get used to not being around people. . . .

The person in prison resents the fact that you aren't frozen in time the way they are. They want you to put your life on hold. They don't want you to be living a life that they aren't living. You have no choice but to be there for them, though. People in prison are often desperate. You have to listen to them talk about how they're going to kill themselves. It tears you up inside. . . . If one person is in jail the entire family is in jail.

And it's not just the immediate family that suffers; when vast numbers of men from the same neighborhood go to prison, the entire community takes a hit. The reason (as argued by Dina Rose and Todd Clear of the John Jay College of Criminal Justice) is that when a neighborhood loses enough men, community stability begins to break down. With a breadwinner in prison, families feel more vulnerable—financially and otherwise. And with men in short supply, the community feels a collective loss of cohesion and control.

Unfortunately, when the men come out—and roughly six hundred thousand inmates are released (into largely poor, urban, nonwhite communities) each year—most of them are ill-equipped to contribute anything of value to the community. As Sister Simone Ponnet of Abraham House observed, "Jail is a school for crime. People don't change, or they change for the worse."

Sure, there is the occasional miracle: the noble figure who uses the time incarcerated to make himself into a better man, who decides (in the biblical spirit of Abraham) to redirect his life toward good. But that, obviously, is not the usual outcome. Instead, people tend to emerge with fewer options than when they went in: They are less employable, angrier, and very much at risk of returning to the same associations and same practices that landed them in the penitentiary in the first place.

It doesn't have to be that way. Garry Mendez of the National Trust believes that with a little support the millions of men involved with the criminal justice system could actually become a force for good. "They are a resource," he insists, and we ought to find a way to use them.

His own work in prisons around the country has convinced him that the process is not necessarily all that difficult. But first, "you have to purge these guys of the value system they've acquired since they got here . . . got to knock this foundation out." He begins by trying to impress upon them that even a prisoner must take responsibility for his family. He tells them, "You have to raise your kids, whether you're locked up or not." He also believes in instilling what he calls "African values," by which he means (among other things) that he tries to get across the message that "crime is not part of our heritage." Mendez even has a dream for what he calls a "liability to an asset fund," the idea being that people in prison would give money for a fund that would help pay for the college education of the children of those who are incarcerated.

Mendez's dream may end up being a bit too utopian for this world. It's hard for me to imagine hundreds of thousands of prisoners coughing up, say, five dollars every few months for a fund to send children to college. But I do think he is right in believing that many of the men we are giving up on could be saved—and could eventually contribute much to society and to their communities. Abraham House and scores of other such programs around the country have demonstrated as much. On a much larger scale, so has Canada.

The Correctional Service of Canada redefined its mandate in the 1980s. It currently sees its job not primarily as punishing people but as safely reintegrating offenders back into the community as law-abiding citizens. Its incarceration rate, significantly higher than in Western Europe, is much lower (roughly one fifth) of that in the United States. Under its philosophy of reintegration, Canada's recidivism rate has dropped to less than half of what it was two decades ago. "If we became harsher . . . we actually think that it would prevent us from dealing with the factors that lead to more offenses later on," Canada corrections commissioner Ole Ingstrup told me. Instead, he advocates what he calls "the restorative model."

In the United States, we have followed the opposite approach. Rather than trying to build prisoners up, we have spent a great deal of energy trying to tear them down. And to a large extent, we have succeeded. But that is an extremely dubious accomplishment. For the vast majority of those imprisoned will come out eventually. And they will be entering an uncertain economy where the so-called social safety net is stretched thinner (partly as a result of welfare reform) than it has been in decades. We are talking, for the most part, about a very young population. Only 10 percent of those in state prisons (and 22 percent in federal facilities) are forty-five or older. Most will hit the streets well before they become too old to do further damage to themselves and to those around them. And since we, as a society, seem determined to make their lives hell, we shouldn't be terribly surprised if they return the favor.

Many communities are already feeling the consequences as thousands of men re-enter communities where there are few productive activities for them to get involved in, where an ex-con is much more likely to be embraced by a gang than by anyone offering a job. And not only is it the so-called hardened criminals we need to worry about, but juvenile offenders as well.

Fed up with so-called superpredators and baby-faced hoods, jurisdictions across America are sending increasing numbers of mostly black and Latino young people into adult prisons. The idea is that these vicious predators have proven themselves so beyond redemption that they deserve whatever evil—from rape to murder—that may befall them in such places. But though their spirits may be broken among hard cons serving hard time, they too will, in virtually every case, eventually emerge into the world, and when they do they will be infinitely more embittered, less caring, and more dangerous than when they went in—all the more so because they cannot help but see that at least part of their crime consisted of being born into the wrong race or ethnic group and happening to live in the wrong neighborhood.

As journalist Alden Loury observed, blacks tend not to get too many breaks when they run afoul of police authority: "I don't know if society ever looks at a black man and says, 'He was young; he made a mistake.' " And statistics bear out that suspicion.

Building Blocks for Youth, an organization that researches criminal justice issues, found that 82 percent of all juveniles sent to adult courts in eighteen jurisdictions across America were members of a racial or ethnic minority group. And 52 percent were black males. Even accounting for the disproportionately large share of crimes that black youths commit, they are much more likely than whites to be condemned to languish in the adult system. As Los Angeles civil rights attorney Connie Rice notes, "You can talk all you want about individual behavior. But you have to recognize that there are different systems for different echelons of society. We incarcerate poor kids for things that middle-class kids get counseling for."

But even setting aside the relatively small numbers of juveniles sent to adult prisons, we still are confronted with a system that stacks the deck against black kids. Earlier, I suggested that it begins with the school system, with teachers and institutions that don't believe most blacks kids can learn. One could argue, however, that it begins even earlier, with the fact that in a society as segregated as ours, black kids are at a much higher risk of being born into a neighborhood where, for a myriad of reasons, the most appealing role models operate outside the law.

Whether or not we agree at what arbitrary point the process of prison preparation begins, we know that it begins very young, and that unless something happens to rescue black children, many who could be saved will be doomed. We also know that every step that takes them closer to darkness—poor schools, incarcerated parents, exile to a juvenile facility—makes it that much less likely that they will find their way into the light.

Even the U.S. Congress, at least rhetorically, has recognized the problem. A 1999 preliminary report to the House Bipartisan Working Group on Youth Violence argued that problem children were, in large measure, the result of problematic home and school environments: "We should . . . use public . . . and visiting nurses to reach out to mothers in need to help them gain the knowledge they need to raise healthy children. We need to teach parents how to parent. And we need to help all children in the pre-school years."

Such stirring words notwithstanding, the path from boyhood to a rewarding adulthood is not getting any easier—not for boys of color, at any rate. The simple fact that a youth is black (particularly if he is poor) radically increases his risk of becoming a target—and ultimately a casualty—of law enforcement. In many poor, urban, minority communities adolescence can be seen less as a time of preparation for college than for eventual confinement.

An analysis in 2001 by a panel from the National Research Council, one of America's most renowned scientific bodies, gives some idea of how racially skewed the criminal justice system has become: "Although black youth represented approximately 15 percent of the U.S. population ages 10-17 in 1997, they represented 26 percent of all juvenile arrests, 30 percent of delinquency referrals to juvenile court, . . . 46 percent of cases judicially waived to adult criminal court, and 40 percent of juveniles in public long-term institutions."

Ideally, the juvenile system would have a restorative mission; it would be a place where lost young souls could receive the guidance that would give them a better shot at a healthy adulthood. But perhaps one reason that it does not is that law enforcement officials tend to believe that our youngsters are not particularly worth saving. The National Research Council found, for instance, that while court officers generally attributed white kids' crimes to "external environmental factors," for black children, "crime was attributed to negative attitudinal traits and personality defects." Given such attitudes, it's hardly surprising, as Useni Eugene Perkins of Chicago points out, that for black males going through a juvenile facility is little more than a rite of passage into an adult prison. And few institutions in our communities have offered effective, large-scale alternatives. Even black churches, for the most part, observes Perkins, have turned inward. They are "more concerned with building bigger churches than building schools for kids."

Fact is, the task may simply be too large for black churches, or any other single institution in our communities. But if we truly care about the future not only of black and Latino males, but of America itself, we have no choice but to try to find a way out of this prison trap that we have managed to build for ourselves.

We have set up an enterprise that helps destroy communities in the name of protecting them, that sets up the most vulnerable, especially blacks and Latinos, for failure and then puts them in shackles when they go wrong, while giving middle-class kids, especially white ones, a second chance at a successful life. It is a system that pushes punishment as an all-purpose solution, but thereby throws countless salvageable souls down the sewer, a system that takes children, at the point where they are both most vulnerable and most amenable to change, and all but condemns them to the life of a thug. It is a system that in three decades has quintupled the number of citizens locked down, a system that (with felony convictions) has stripped four million Americans of the right to vote (including one eighth of all black men in the United States), while tossing more and more tax dollars at private corporations to build and maintain even more prisons to keep ever growing numbers of Americans under lock and key. We, who stood up to slavery and lynchings, who threw off the indignities of Jim Crow, who demanded our rights at the risk of our lives, are now surrendering those very rights with barely a whimper as we march, en masse, to jail. Such ironies are killing us!

There is much that we can do to turn things around. Among the most important may be showing young people—young men in particular—that there are better things to plan for in life than a stay in the penitentiary. A former hustler and drug dealer made the point plainly. "We don't know what options we have," he told me. "We don't have people to tell us what living is about." Garry Mendez of the National Trust makes much the same point: "We as adults, the seniors, have not told the junior members of the community what we expect of them. . . . They think they're on their own, and they are."

Kirkland Vaughans, my psychologist friend, has noticed something similar: Many black men don't talk to their sons about their own lives; they don't share their experiences and traumas with racism and therefore don't prepare their children for the hardships (and possible triumphs) of life: "The black boys don't have the sense of the world in which their fathers lived. [And there is little] emotional understanding of each other's life." Consequently, there is a breakdown of intergenerational empathy—and a diminished parental ability to educate.

It is not just that we have been remiss in telling young people about our own experiences and expectations; we have been even more remiss in showing them what is possible, in exposing them to the kinds of experiences that will inspire them to grow, that allowed a young Franklin Raines, for instance, to see a world—and a set of options—so much larger than those in the 'hood. We the seniors, as Mendez calls us, have done a poor job in offering a more compelling vision of life to many youngsters than the one offered by the neighborhood drug dealer. Obviously, if those young souls are to survive, we must do better.

We also must become better at critiquing this entire, immense, and extremely flawed system that has funneled so many of our young into penal institutions. We must become better at convincing politicians who profit from their cynicism that throwing more and more teenagers and troubled young men into jail is neither in their or in our society's best interest. We must become better, in short, at making the argument that somewhere, between coddling wrongdoers and destroying their spirit, lies a better way.

No one with much sense would argue that every criminal heart turned cold can be thawed, that every soul neglected or made cruel by experience can be rescued. But unless we are prepared to either kill prisoners outright or lock them up forever, we ultimately have no choice but to re-embrace some concept of human reclamation, if not for their sakes, for the sake of our communities, to which most eventually will return. Those communities, we are just beginning to realize, have been punished nearly as much by America's fixation on prison as have the criminals our political leaders decided were incapable of reform.

* * *

A few days before Christmas 2000 I stopped by a Manhattan criminal courtroom to watch a prosecutor friend deliver the closing argument in a case that had consumed him for nearly two years. The friend was prosecuting Arohn Malik Kee, a black man in his twenties indicted for murdering, mutilating, raping, and robbing several black and Latina teens in Harlem over a period of less than eight years.

The first girl raped and strangled was Paola Illera, a thirteen-year-old Colombian immigrant who left for school in January 1991 and never made it home. The second murder victim, nineteen-year-old Johalis Castro, a Dominican, was raped and killed in 1997 before being doused in gasoline and burned beyond easy recognition. ("A conscious attempt to destroy her, to destroy her identity," my prosecutor friend told the jury.) The last murder victim was Rasheda Washington, eighteen, black, an aspiring fashion designer who was raped, strangled and left in a stairwell in 1998. Kee also had been indicted for raping and sodomizing four other teenaged girls who somehow had managed to escape with their lives.

Several years earlier—nearly four years before a SWAT team burst in on Kee in a shabby Florida hotel where he had fled with a fifteen-year-old Brooklyn girl who professed to love him—Kee had complained (in comments unrelated to his murder case) to the New York *Daily News* about police racism: "It's a big issue to black people. I am tired of being stereotyped because I wear baggy pants and I'm black."

What eventually became extraordinarily clear is that if racism had anything at all to do with Kee's treatment, it was a racism that worked to his advantage. Because he preyed on blacks and Latinas, his assaults, though not exactly ignored, were never the focus of much attention.

As John Irwin, the prosecutor and a former Georgetown University varsity basketball player, walked into the courtroom, I noticed that he seemed more gaunt, more tightly wound than I had seen him previously, physical manifestations, I assumed, of the pressure generated by the case, pressure that derived not just from the drive to win—which he assumed that he would, particularly given DNA evidence that essentially proved Kee was the perpetrator—but by getting to know the victims' parents, by, in effect, becoming their champion. He now carried much of the weight of their anguished expectations.

We chatted briefly as Irwin made his way to the prosecutors' table. He had no intention of showboating, he said: "When semen is in the victim's vagina, there's no point in oratory. Soaring rhetoric is simply not necessary."

True to his word, when he addressed the jury, Irwin let the facts speak for themselves. "This case is as straightforward and simple as it seems to be," he explained to the jurors, and methodically demolished what feeble defense (including a rambling statement from the witness chair by Kee) had been offered.

Through much of the closing statement, Kee, who fancied himself a computer whiz and rap promoter, tinkered with his lawyer's laptop computer. At one point, apparently fed up with the nasty things being said about him, he asked the judge whether he could leave the room. "You're better off sitting here, taking it like a man, so to speak," she replied. So he sat there, fidgeting, and finally coiled his body around the table, an altogether pathetic figure, with short hair, an olive-colored suit, and a pained expression.

A slender, attractive young woman near the front of the courtroom kept her eyes on him the entire time. Someone later told me she was an admirer, perhaps one of the girl-friends that, until his trial, Kee always seem to have in abundant supply. My attention was more strongly drawn, however, to a number of spectators near the back, all of whom seemed to be in mourning. One woman, who I presumed to be Washington's mother, broke into tears as Irwin described how Kee had squeezed the girl's body into a shopping cart before leaving her in the stairwell.

A few days later, Kee was convicted of all the major charges. At his sentencing—something of a formality, since the verdicts guaranteed he would never be free again—the agony of the victims spilled out in heated outburst, and Kee's own mother begged him to apologize.

Later, over lunch, I asked Irwin what he made of the case, and he talked of how close he had gotten to some of the parents, of how sitting in the victims' corner "can erase a certain cynicism that certain segments of communities of color have toward the criminal justice system."

We talked as well about the relative lack of press coverage for the case compared to that of Nicole Barrett, a young white woman who had moved to New York from East Texas and was attacked in late 1999 by a man wielding a brick. Though Barrett's injuries were serious, she survived the attack and eventually recovered—unlike several of Kee's victims. Nonetheless, while Barrett's case was covered by a huge press corps and was front-page news for several days running, the girls murdered by Kee largely were ignored by the press. At Kee's sentencing, when some reporters finally did show up, Rasheda Washington's father exploded in frustration:

"Where were they in the beginning?" he asked, apparently referring to both the police and the press. "It took another two girls to get raped for them to do anything? . . . It's because they're black and Hispanic! It's because it's all above Ninety-sixth Street! Let there be a white girl, and it's solved within days!"

Gregory Washington had a point, observed Irwin. When whites, especially middle-class whites, are victims of heinous crimes, immense resources and press coverage have a way of materializing, whereas the atrocities committed against the black and Latina girls of Harlem barely raised the city's collective temperature. Obviously, in many eyes, the lives of ordinary blacks are not quite as precious as those of ordinary whites.

Irwin also made another observation: "Arohn Kee is evil, but he is the great exception. . . . Most people who are in jail are not such bad people; but for the fact that most of those people were born into the communities they were born into, they would not be in jail."

For weeks afterward, my mind periodically went back to the trial, attempting to sort out all I had seen and heard. Kee's depravity was simply beyond my comprehension as was the thinking of women (such as the one who showed up to support him at trial) who knowingly attach themselves to such malevolent men. One point that Kee makes very clear, however, is that some people truly belong in prison, that the old argument, made most notably by the Black Panthers, that incarcerated blacks are *all* political prisoners is just so much nonsense.

Politicians get a great deal of mileage out of pretending that virtually any defendant (white-collar criminals and fellow politicians excepted) is a potential Arohn Kee—unregenerate, unrepentant, wicked, vile. I happen to believe that Irwin's point is much closer to the truth—that unhealthy circumstances, more so than inherent evil, is what lands so many of our young people behind bars. My fear is that unless we as a society come to grips with that basic reality, we will create more of the very monsters that we most fear, by condemning more and more souls that could have been saved to prisons, where their only choice is to mold themselves in the image of those who are truly beyond redemption.

5

Of Relationships, Fatherhood, and Black Men

I had lived in Washington, D.C., less than a year when she called to let me know she was moving to town and would love to get together for dinner. She was a broadcast journalist I had met a few years earlier, and with whom I had forged a casual friendship; and now, as she prepared for her big career move, she wanted my input as she took the lay of the land. More specifically, she wanted to know what to expect as an attractive, successful, single black woman who was preparing to enter a town she had heard was romantically inhospitable to women like herself, a town where the odds were so skewed (she had heard the ratio of available black women to men was something like ten to one) that even ugly, shiftless, useless brothers had their pick of desirable women.

Before I could respond to her open-ended questions, she proceeded to tell me a story. It seems that a female friend of hers, also successful, had advised her that Washington men were absolute "dogs" and that the only way to deal with them was to surrender your heart to no one. Instead, it was best to keep two or three on a string, the idea being that, if one fell through, another was always in reserve to promptly take his place.

I suspect I was not much help since, as I readily admitted, her concerns were far beyond my meager expertise. I did, however, over the course of our meal, offer what I hoped were a couple of helpful observations. The ten-to-one ratio was simply absurd, I said, since even a cursory review of census data would reveal it to be nothing more than a myth. And as for the impossibility of finding love, I told her, I knew of several women in town who seemed to be in mutually fulfilling heterosexual liaisons. My friend seemed far from reassured.

Some years later, after moving to New York, I had a similar conversation with another female friend. She was then in her early thirties, attractive, well educated, and held a prestigious position in a major New York institution. Her problem, she confided, was that she could not find a man. And among her peers, she was not alone. It seems that she knew many women, more or less like herself, who had no serious romantic relationship and were mystified as to why. The fault, she concluded, lay with black men, who "go out with Asians, whites, Hispanic women, everybody but us."

That black men and black women have *issues* between us is nothing if not an understatement. You could probably decorate a fair-sized dungeon with the titles devoted to our so-called war. Nearly a quarter of a century ago, in *Black Macho and the Myth of the Superwoman,* which now rates as something of a black feminist classic, Michele Wallace declared, "[For] perhaps the last fifty years there has been a growing distrust, even hatred, between black men and black women. It has been nursed along not only by racism on the part of whites but also by an almost deliberate ignorance on the part of blacks about the sexual politics of their experience in this country."

More recently, in a book provocatively titled *Do Black Women Hate Black Men?* psychologist A. L. Reynolds III analyzed what he called "a war between the genders." Not *all* black women hate black men, he acknowledged, "but too many black women have been hurt, abused, abandoned, left pregnant, helpless, and homeless by black men who refuse to accept responsibility for their marriages or their relationships."

Clearly there are some very serious tensions between individual black men and black women; there are also tensions between black men and black women as groups. I have never, however, thought that "war" properly described the dynamic. War implies, among other things, that there is a finite and defined struggle, that there eventually can be a winner and a loser, and that some important principle or valuable property sits at the center of the dispute. I think what is happening between black men and women is infinitely more complicated than a war, and partly for that reason, impossible to categorize simply.

Let me begin, however, with two observations: Though interracial marriage rates are increasing rapidly, the vast majority of black men and women (well over 90 percent) still choose to live with, marry, date, or mate with others of their own race. (The U.S. Census's Bureau 1998 Current Population Reports, for instance, noted that black-white interracial married couples were well under 1 percent of all married couples.) People truly at war would not be so eager to hook up with one another.

Second, most of the bad things many black men are accused of doing to black women they seem also to do to other women, which is simply another way of saying that what is often characterized as behavior directed at black women is just the way some black men treat *all* women— which is to say that the dialogue on black-white, male-female relations has racialized many things that are not really racial in any meaningful sense.

Let me make a third observation—one that is rather damning to those of us who are black men. By virtually any criteria of what constitutes good behavior, when it comes to women and children, we as a group are guilty of just about everything of which we stand accused. And we damn well know it, which is one of the reasons Louis Farrakhan found it so easy to gather hundreds of thousands of us in the District of Columbia in 1995 for what was essentially a feel-good day of momentary atonement.

In *What's Love Got to Do with It?*, sociologist Donna L. Franklin argues that relationships between black men and women "are in crisis." Relying on a variety of data sources, she reports that black men are more confrontational with their wives than white men; that violence (and it goes both ways) between black men and women is higher than for other races; that reported rates of infidelity are higher for black men than for whites; and that black men seem to be more demanding of—and less satisfied with—the women they have married. (Black married women, it should be noted, are not particularly happy with their men or marriages, either.)

When I asked Franklin about her research during a leisurely afternoon coffee in Santa Monica, she elaborated on some of the things that she believes has brought the crisis about. For one thing, she said, black men and women suffered from unfounded suspicions and misinformation—so much so that it is "difficult for us to find solace with each other." She had picked up feelings of estrangement on the part of black men, feelings that seemed to derive from a sense that in a racially charged society such as ours, black women had an unfair advantage. Black women supposedly are getting jobs black men should be getting and are somehow "in cahoots with the white community." On many levels, the suspicion is absurd, for the data that Franklin is so very familiar with clearly indicate that black men who are working earn, on average, more money than black women. But there is more than simple ignorance fueling the anxiety.

Black male managers outnumber black women by nearly 20 percent, but the male advantage vanishes when it comes to the so-called professions. Among black professionals—people working in occupations "requiring either college graduation or experience of such kind and amount as to provide a comparable background," as defined by the U.S. government—women greatly outnumber men. For every 100 black males so employed, there are 183 black women, according to statistics collected in 1999 by the U.S. Equal Employment Opportunity Commission. This is not even remotely true with any other group. Among whites, Hispanics, and Asian Americans roughly equal numbers of men and women work as professionals.

The gap between professional black men and women has not always been so large. Although black women outnumbered men in such jobs twenty years ago, the gap was one fourth the size that it is now. The change is clearly linked to the fact that black women are increasingly more likely than black men to graduate from college. And to the extent that young black women continue to be more college-oriented than men, the disparity will increase.

But the hard feelings Franklin is picking up must rest in something deeper, more psychologically profound, than the growing inequality between black men and black women when it comes to credentials for—and likelihood of getting into—certain careers. Part of the suspicion, she believes, stems from the age many decades ago when educated women could get jobs as teachers while educated black men were left out in the cold. Even today, she believes, many employers are more likely to hire black women than men—if only because, to many whites, black women seem less threatening.

Other factors also contribute to the tension, in Franklin's view. One is the much discussed phenomenon of the shortage of desirable, marriageable men. Some 50 percent of black men, she said, claim to be unable to find a suitable mate, compared to 20 percent of white men. Why? "When numbers are that skewed, you get pickier?" Yet, at the same time black men are getting pickier, black women—at least well-educated, employed black women—are getting more assertive. "As women get more income, they're not taking shit," says Franklin. Throw in the fact that black men register very high on "male dominance ideology" scales—that we, in other words, tend to feel that we men ought to be in charge—and you have a prescription for conflict. Partly for that reason, speculates Franklin, black women from selective schools have twice the divorce rate of their white, female classmates.

Are desirable black men really so difficult to find? If by desirable, we mean well-educated men without criminal records with good employment prospects who will stay around to see their children grow to adulthood, the obvious answer is "yes." We certainly are rarer than black women who have those particular attributes—at least among the younger generations. If we look at all black men and women above the age of 25, educational achievement levels are more or less comparable: 36.5 percent of black men older than 25 are high school graduates compared to 35.3 percent of black women; 12.5 percent of men older than 25 have bachelor's degrees compared to 13.9 percent of women. But when we look only at those between the ages of 25 and 34, ages that some consider the prime marriage years, the differences become dramatic, at least at the college level. Whereas only 11.9 percent of black men have bachelor's degrees, 15.6 percent of black women do. Put another way, women of that age are more than 30 percent more likely to have earned at least a bachelor's degree than black men. And when we consider the fact that there are significantly more black women than black men in the population, the disparity becomes even greater. (We tend to die earlier for any number of reasons. One, noted previously, is that we are literally killing one another.) For every black man in that age range who holds a bachelor's or more advanced degree, there are 1.6 black women—and that is not even accounting for the hundreds of thousands of men with felony records or in prison. The disparity is not quite as huge for those between the ages of 35 and 44, but it is still disconcertingly large.

What that means quite simply is that if a well-educated young black woman wants a well-educated young black man, she is facing some fairly formidable odds, and might be well advised to broaden her horizons. In light of such numbers, it's hardly surprising that so many myths have sprouted, that many black women sincerely believe that there are scarcely any "good men" left, or believe that there are ten women for every "decent" man. Nor is it surprising that the behavior of many black men and women is shaped, in some fundamental way, by such beliefs. Many of us (men, that is) have developed an arrogance when it comes to the opposite sex, and consequently behave in ways that make many women feel extremely angry and insecure.

It is not merely our arrogance, however, that is behind much of the anger and frustration; it is also the sense, as my friend put it, that we prize women of other races above our own. In the same way that many straight women believe that most of the "best" men are gay, many black women in search of a mate now believe most desirable brothers are off chasing "Miss Ann."

First, let me repeat my earlier observation: Black men are much more likely to end up with a black woman than with a women of another race (and this is true irrespective of education or social class). Black men are also much more likely to end up with women of their own ethnicity than are Asian Americans, Latinos, Native Americans, Filipinos, or members of virtually any other ethnic group that reside in the United States. (Roughly a third of Puerto Ricans and Mexicans in the United States are married to people out-side their ethnic group. And the number goes even higher for Asian Americans and Native Americans.) Let me also make the point that I personally have never felt race to be among the most important criteria in choosing a partner, that I believe—and always have—that we (human beings, that is) are fortunate to find love and a decent relationship wherever we find it, regardless of that person's race, ethnic ancestry, or, for that matter, sexual orientation. All that being said, let me add that only a fool—or someone totally ignorant of America's history—would blame black women for being hurt or upset when *their men* go off with women of other races. Much of this nation's history has consisted of abusing, exploiting, and raping black women, while simultaneously declaring them undesirable and unworthy. So the last thing any black women needs to hear from a black man is that her race renders her undesirable to him.

When I raised the issue of interracial relationships with Donna Franklin, she made a characteristically pithy observation: "Your experience is one of wanting it; ours is one of saying 'Get out of here.' " There was also, she added, the fact that, going all the way back to slavery times, many black women (due to the ill treatment they received) have felt bitterness toward white women, so to see *those women* walking off with black men understandably causes some black women to seethe. Making the situation even more complicated is the sexual power white society (including white women) often attributes to the black male. "You all are idealized in a way that we aren't," notes Franklin. And the evidence of that idealization is, more than ever, out in the open.

Americans have moved far beyond the point when Sidney Poitier or Harry Belafonte could damn near cause a race riot merely by touching a white woman on stage. These days we have become so racially sophisticated that we just watch in bemusement as Jerry Springer presides over a daily circus where white women are apt to threaten bodily harm to each other because of jealousy over a (generally smirking) black male. What it all is supposed to mean, I guess, is that we finally have become very casual about interracial relations, that we are beyond the stage of being shocked by black and white sex. And in some sense that is true; having finally legalized "miscegenation," Americans have been forced to accept the idea that black-white couples exist. But to assume that Americans have so quickly gotten over the irrational preoccupations that got black men lynched for even seeming to lust after white flesh would be to assume we are far freer of our past than we typically have proven to be. Certainly, if the O. J. and Nicole Simpson tragedy proved nothing else, it proved that Americans are not very capable of ignoring the sexual-racial fissures rooted in our history.

I recall being reminded just how powerful sexual-racial fixations can be, even in the most liberal of circles, during my first trip to New York, a city I assumed to be the most sophisticated in the nation. My visit had no particular purpose. I had simply decided, having turned twenty-one, that I should see the most exciting city in the United States. And not knowing a soul, I asked a friend—a native New Yorker—for an introduction to someone who might be interesting company. He suggested an old buddy and, upon arriving in Manhattan, I called the man, who insisted on coming to my hotel and picking me up immediately.

The man turned out to be an extremely charming West Indian—an accountant by day and a hipster by night, with an eclectic assortment of friends (mostly white, female, and, for the most part, foreign) who roamed in and out of his home at all hours of the day and night, often enveloped in a cloud of marijuana smoke. One morning, as some members of his female posse prepared breakfast, I overheard what for me, at that age, was a fascinating discussion. They were speaking in quite graphic terms, evaluating the sexual differences, from penis size to love-making technique, between black and white men, and of their intention to go clubbing that evening in hopes of finding (for lack of a better term) chocolate delight. (As I recall, black men were supposedly larger, rougher and had smoother skin.) Their voices were a mixture of frivolity and excitement, reflecting, I suppose, the thrill of the upcoming hunt. The conversation stayed with me long after I had left New York, not only because it seemed so utterly bizarre but because I had never heard such a graphic discussion among women that reduced black men to nothing more than sex toys.

That, of course, was way back in the seventies, when a lot of black men and a lot of white women were feverishly experimenting with the previously forbidden, when Jim Crow was not a distant memory but a grand cornerstone of the national psyche. It was a time when the nation was just awakening from a sort of self-created mental illness, an era only a generation removed from a period of moral madness so profound that sex between a black man and a white woman literally had been cause for murder. To recall how truly insane that epoch was, that point in history before the civil rights struggle stirred the conscience of America, you need only read the passage in *No Name in the Street* where James Baldwin describes his tortured relationship with a certain blonde. The two of them would never leave the house together; she would leave alone and he would follow. They would meet on a subway platform and pretend not to know each other and they would leave the subway, separately, and walk, again separately, to their destination—all the while fearing the consequences of being found out. "She was far safer walking the streets alone than walking with me—a brutal and humiliating fact which thoroughly destroyed whatever relationship this girl and I might have been able to achieve," wrote Baldwin. It's difficult to imagine a black man and white woman in today's Manhattan

(the situation in some of the outer boroughs, you understand, may be different) having to endure such madness,
having to skulk around in fear for their lives, simply to pursue a relationship. These days interracial relationships are
so common that they raise fewer eyebrows, in certain
places, than would a pair of two-tone shoes. We are, in so
many ways, so far removed from that dark time in history.
But we are not so far removed as many Americans like to
think. We (meaning Americans) still have this thing with
interracial sex; and we (meaning black men) are as suscepti-
ble as any.

This digression is by way of reinforcing a point: Color
considerations have not disappeared, and they still have
something to do with relations between black women and
men. There are still many of us who are somewhat color-
struck; who, in the Jim Crow past, would not have dared
approach a white woman, but who had a definite preference for lighter-skinned blacks. In this new age, when many
racial barriers have fallen, that preference plays itself out in
somewhat expanded ways.

My younger sister, LaVerne, at one point confided that
she had stopped watching black music videos because she
rarely saw women like herself: All the women on display,
dancing away, were several shades lighter than she, and it
pained her to think that that was the only desirable black
female image that video makers could see.

Allison Samuels, a *Newsweek* colleague who covers
(among other things) hip-hop and sports, made the same
point in much stronger terms. Not only had she noticed
that rappers were not using many dark-skinned women in
their videos, but they seemed to be shying away from using
identifiably black women altogether. They had a definite

preference, in her opinion, for Latina and Asian women, for women with "long, silky hair, the . . . body type. . . . Blacker-than-thou rappers, how they let this happen, I don't under-stand," she grumbled.

She had noticed the same preference among black profes-sional athletes. Once upon a time when she would go to an NBA party, almost all of the women were black. Nowadays there seemed to be more Hispanics and Filipinas, and black athletes appeared to welcome the change. "I'm still with a minority, so you [meaning black women] can't get mad at me," their attitude seemed to say.

Seeing such successful black men go crazy over light-skinned women brought back painful memories from her predominantly black college. She'd had two close friends who were light-skinned and had soon learned that "guys would knock me over to get to them." Eventually, for her own piece of mind, she decided to stop hanging out with them. She also recalled a male friend who had told her, "You would be cute if you weren't so dark." And though she had managed a witty comeback ("You would be smart, if you weren't so stupid"), the memory still rankled.

What rankled also was that it was the most successful black men who seemed so obsessed with escaping black women: "Not necessarily Jamal and Jamil in the projects. It's those guys who got out of the projects."

Her experience dating a well-known rap artist had only confirmed her impressions about the preferences of so many black men. One day a friend of his, unaware that she was listening, told the rapper, "You don't usually date someone who looks like [her]." "I think he felt a certain amount of pressure," she confided, to get out of the rela-tionship. In her opinion the color complex was "not what really broke us up, but it was one of the reasons." He needed a trophy and, solely because of her complexion, she did not fit the bill.

In the scheme of things, intraracial color issues are not the biggest reason that it's "difficult for us to find solace with each other," as Donna Franklin put it. But they show how we are still wrestling with the demons of another age and time, demons imposed upon us by a society that makes us doubt our own value—and, consequently, doubt the worth of our kind. They show how difficult it has been for us, men and women alike, decades after we declared that "black is beautiful," to accept, within our hearts, that those simple words might actually be true. And they show how the struggle with questions of self-acceptance and self-worth continue to touch so many aspects of our lives; for the larger issue is not simply the persistence of color discrimination, but of conflict rooted in some fundamental unhappiness with our collective selves.

Why do black men and women batter each other more than whites? The research data offers no easy answer. Nor is it totally consistent. Some surveys suggest that for those of us in certain income brackets, spousal abuse is not any more of a problem than it is for other groups. A large research review by Carolyn M. West, of the Family Research Laboratory at the University of New Hampshire, led her to conclude that black couples, particularly those under thirty, have significantly more violence between them than whites, largely because huge numbers of blacks who were blue collar or unemployed were driving the numbers up. I'm not sure exactly what those findings mean, but to me they imply that a great deal of the conflict—of the violence—stems from frustrations black men are having because we are not doing better in life, because we see ourselves blocked from serving the man of the house role to which we attach such great importance—more importance, apparently, than white men. So, in extreme cases, we attempt to relieve those frustrations by beating up on our mates.

It would, of course, be simplistic—and wrong—to try to reduce all our problems, all the conflicts we have as black women and men, to issues of self-esteem or self-worth. There are some other huge problems, and perhaps none is larger than those that revolve around abandonment; and by abandonment, I don't mean the abandonment of black women for white women, but the abandonment of children.

Today the vast majority of black children don't live with both parents. A few decades ago that was not the case. In 1960, just over two thirds of black children under the age of eighteen lived in a household with two parents. By 1991, the percentage had dropped to just over one third—and has continued going down since. The implications of that are staggering. For what it means, among other things, is that a lot of black children—more than ever—feel that at least one parent, generally the father, has abandoned them. And the mother often is so stressed out simply trying to survive that she is overwhelmed by—and therefore inadequate to perform properly—the extraordinarily consuming job of good parenting.

A successful black woman who, by her own admission, has had a series of disastrous relationships, tried to explain to me what had gone wrong with her love life. "When your first man leaves you, what happens?" she asked, rhetorically. "You become sexually active at an early age. . . . You go looking for love with men, older men [who are only] looking for sex. . . . When you are never made to feel special, you settle."

Only after years of personal chaos, she said, had she finally managed to find someone who made her feel "special."

What such abandonment also can mean is that some children never form an image of what a successful male-female relationship looks like, so they essentially accept abuse as a normal part of life. As another woman I raised the subject with put it: "If you get used to something, that feels normal to you.... Even today I can't tell a normal man from an abusive man."

For boys raised without a father (or any other appropriate male figure) the problems can be just as huge. In the worst case those boys end up adopting some supermacho image of masculinity, asserting their manhood by brutalizing other people (particularly the women) in their lives.

This is not to say that people raised by single parents cannot turn out just fine. In fact, most do very well. But it is to say that, in many cases, the absence of a parent can be one of many factors contributing to an unhealthy attitude about relationships. And, in addition to the many other pressures we face in our communities, the absence of a healthy male figure can often be *the* crucial factor when it comes to our emotional health.

The rapid increase in fatherless households, I should note, is not peculiar to blacks. White families are experiencing the same phenomenon, though they have not yet reached the level that we see in our community. As Donna Franklin observed, "White families are where black families were [a few decades ago]." Put another way, the problems caused by fatherlessness are in no way racial—it is just that, like so many problems in this society, they happen to hit us harder.

The same, in fact, could be said of drugs. One survey

after another has shown that drug usage among whites and blacks is more or less equivalent. But white communities were never devastated by crack, as were many of ours; and, again, the consequences for black-female relationships have been catastrophic.

"Crack wiped out the nurturers. . . . It was stronger than motherhood," says Joe Marshall, of the Omega Boys Club, who blames the addiction of mothers to crack for the neglect of many black boys. Untold numbers of those boys, many of whom now are men, were never taught to respect or care for women. They were taught the opposite—that women are things to be used, objects unworthy of respect. As Damion Samuels of the Harlem Educational Activities Fund observed: "The crack generation saw so many women out in the street, looking terrible, doing anything [to score crack]." Such behavior inevitably had some effect on how the young boys observing it came to see women.

Mimi Silbert, founder of a San Francisco–based program that has helped thousands of one-time addicts rebuild their lives, made a similar observation. Three decades ago, when the Delancey Street Foundation started, the typical client was a first-generation drug abuser. Now she is seeing second- and third-generation addicts: "The grandmother may be part of the [drug] life, may be waiting to see what the son is bringing home."

Obviously, when a grandmother or a mother is counting on her teenage son's drug money to supplement (or make up the lion's share of) the household budget, when a child has, in effect, become the man of the house—a sort of surrogate husband—the effects not only on the parent-child relationship but on any women that young man happens to be involved with can be catastrophic. Caught up in an emotionally stunting child-husband relationship with his mother, he is unlikely to accept the additional responsibility of raising the children he may be fathering out of wedlock. He is also unlikely to have much of an idea of what a healthy, mature male-female relationship looks like.

Why do some young black men see women as "bitches and hos"? I suspect that at least part of the answer has to do with crack.

None of this is by way of excusing current behaviors, or trying to explain them away as signs of the time. (This is not, after all, the first generation whose men sometimes see women as things. Eldridge Cleaver clearly did. The very fact that a so-called black revolutionary group could embrace a man who "practiced" rape on black women says volumes about the misogyny that has long existed in our midst.) It is, however, to say that in the last few years some unhealthy traits have found strong reinforcement—and female-male relationships have suffered for that.

Something else, obviously, also has happened in the last few years. Somehow the notion got planted in a lot of heads that black men and women are at war. And so the game-playing that has always been part of the male-female mating dance seems to have risen to a new level, and so has the cynicism.

In Philadelphia, with Professor Elijah Anderson, I visited CBC (Campus Boulevard Corporation) Career Institute, a group that helps to train people to get off welfare, and listened to a class discussion, much of which focused on male-female relationships. One woman after another described relationships with men who, instead of supporting their efforts to improve their lives, were trying to tear them down, men who, as one woman put it, "don't want you to succeed. . . . You get to a point where you get tired. I can do bad by myself."

More and more black women are deciding to go it alone—or to look beyond the black community for suitable mates, or to see men principally as providers of sperm, as so many see themselves. In her conversations with fathers who had children by more than one woman, Donna Franklin found the men had a common rationale: "They [the women] wanted the children, and we went along with it."

Some of the women, Franklin suggested, were perhaps being disingenuous: "I think the women want to have children *and* they see having the children as a hook [to get a man]." There is "a fear in our community," she observed, a fear that "I will not have a man and I will not have children." And that fear can sometimes lead to desperate measures. I know of more than one case where a woman has actively tried to get pregnant while pretending to be using contraception. More often than not (whether the man knowingly cooperates as a sperm donor or not) the strategy backfires, leaving the women not only feeling angry and abandoned but with a child for whom the father feels little responsibility. There is nothing at all specifically black about such behavior. It is just that, as with so much else, we seem to suffer from it more.

When it comes to black men and women, as I pointed out earlier, there is no end to the issues between us. There is also a great deal of love, and there is a shared history and an intertwined destiny that cannot be denied. We are part of each other—bound to each other—in more ways than we can ever find time to dispute. On an individual level, we (many of us, anyway) will work our issues out; that after all is what people who care about each other do. In the aggregate—well,

that is a much more complicated matter. Love doesn't necessarily conquer all. And though life would be easier all
around if we all could somehow shake free of our racial-
relationship baggage, I'm not convinced there is any easy
road to intergender, intraracial harmony. I am certainly not
so naïve as to believe our problems can be solved with
another march on Washington, nor am I enough of a fool to
see much point in assigning blame or fault. And I'm not
about to deliver any lecture on morality. I don't believe relationship conflicts and domestic heartache can be addressed
by Moses coming down from Mount Sinai with commandments on commitment. I think relationships take hard—
and very individual—work. In the end, people figure out
what kind of energy to put into them and whether, ultimately, they are worth the effort to make them worthwhile.
But I will make this observation: Virtually everyone agrees in
theory that children should not be pawns in adults' games.
When the Village Foundation commissioned its poll, it
found blacks were much more likely than whites (70.1 percent compared to 57.5 percent) to claim having a father in
the home was important. And as Gary Mendez discovered
with his poll, even the vast majority of black prisoners claim
to want to be part of their children's lives.

There are a million reasons why adults may not get along,
but there is no good reason for abandoning a child. I wonder
whether black men and women have spent so much time
focused on our pain, and so much energy blaming each other,
that we have spent far too little effort sorting out what is best
for the youngsters so many of us bring into the world. I also
wonder whether, if we could somehow figure out a way to put
their interests above our relatively petty concerns, we might
not, in the end, do a better job of taking care of each other.

6

Twelve Things You Must Know to Survive and Thrive in America

There were periods in the weeks after Fred Hampton died when, for moments at a time, the world seemed to stop long enough to allow for mournful reflection on a young life senselessly taken. To my teenaged brain (and to most of black Chicago), the basic facts were reasonably clear, if quite different from the then official version of things. On December 4, 1969, in the dead of night, the Chicago police had broken through a door in a West Side apartment and gunned down the head of Chicago's Black Panther party, along with Mark Clark, his comrade in arms, firing some two hundred bullets in the process.

The Old South, I had never experienced. So my impression of lynchings and of the people who participated in them was simultaneously graphic and vague. But Hampton's execution (which is how my friends and I defined the event), which had taken place only blocks away from my home, was painfully tangible and disturbingly close. It left my head reeling for months.

To me, the execution said volumes about the value of

black male life in America, about how easily people could justify extinguishing it. But it also said a lot about fear: fear of the righteous anger of young, black men; fear of the potential power, bubbling beneath the system, in the alienated hearts of the dispossessed.

During that era (and not only among impressionable teenagers) there was a sense that the so-called system might collapse of its own weight, and that proud black men would rise from the ashes of revolution to take our proper place in the world. Like many young people at the time, I was enthralled by the revolutionary rhetoric, in somewhat the same way, I suppose, that teenagers of another generation were enthralled by rock and roll, or, more recently, rap. But there was a huge part of my mind that never quite bought the message in its entirety. For though I liked the leather jackets and the strutting machismo and the idea (as the popular phrase had it) of speaking *truth* to power, I was never convinced that large parts of the oratory had much to do with truth. I never thought, for one thing, that making a revolution would be quite as easy as some of my more fanciful friends believed. I always detected a large dose of self-delusion in the talk of a grand uprising that would wash away centuries of accumulated chauvinism, a proletariat upheaval so atypical, so extraordinary that it could "not be televised."

And then there was part of me that questioned whether many of the self-declared revolutionaries were quite as revolutionary as they thought, whether they had really managed to purge their minds of the presumptions behind the stereotypes that we all so thoroughly abhorred, whether they, in other words, had shaken free of their awe of the white man's mind.

I recall sitting more than once in an audience and cring-
ing as a speaker, typically resplendent in afro and multicol-
ored dashiki, railed on and on about the deviousness of the
white man. The white man had turned blacks into drug
addicts. ("You don't see no brother flying heroin into
America. Brothers ain't running those big cartels.") The
white man had forced blacks into criminality. The white
man had confused our minds. The white man, it seemed,
was plotting constantly, and with great success, to make
complete fools of us as he pursued his objective of keeping
us in our place. (With Nigerians Abeni and Oluwole
Ogungbuyi making the White House's first international
drug kingpin list in 2000, the notion that "brothers" cannot be international drug lords may, for better or worse, at
last be put to rest.)

While I was prepared to believe some pretty ugly things
about the white man (at least in the abstract and in the
aggregate and with requisite exceptions for my close white
friends), I was not prepared to believe that we were simply
white folks' puppets, that we were so weak-willed, so pow-
erless, so lacking in the ability to exercise critical thought
that we had become mere playthings to the all-powerful
white power structure. For me, that argument posed a vex-
ing paradox: If we really were as pathetic, as superficial, as
blind as some of our would-be revolutionaries made us
sound, why in the world would the white man waste every
waking moment trying to keep us down?

I never heard an explanation that made any sense. Nor
could I believe that anyone (including white anyones)
could manipulate my life so totally. Most of the white
people I knew didn't act like devious gods pulling black
folks' strings; they were pretty ordinary, often insecure,

fallible human beings—and much more preoccupied with their own lives than with anything the black community might be up to.

Don't misunderstand me. I am not saying that racism has no power. And I emphatically disagree with those self-styled conservatives who argue, in effect, that all the problems black people face are of our own doing, or that there is some cultural sickness rampant among African Americans that leads many of us to our doom. Certainly, many of us do extremely self-destructive things. But to see any of those things as indicative of some independently evolved black culture (as opposed to as an indication of some unhealthy ways of coping with past and present racism in American society) would be to misunderstand both U.S. history and human psychology.

It would likewise be a mistake on our part to see racism as an all-powerful force over which we simply don't stand a chance. Too often some of us become so beleaguered with the challenges of life, so overwhelmed by the obstacles (many of them rooted in things racial) tossed in our paths, that we, in effect, shut down and attribute our defeat to that all-powerful, ruthless, elusive enemy known as white society. Or we give in to our more base inclinations and claim we had no choice.

I'm reminded of a drug dealer I met in Philadelphia. When I asked him why he was dealing drugs, he replied that the white man had left him few other options. He wanted nice things, he wanted to attract women, and he had to earn money to accomplish his goals. So he took the only well-paying job the white world had left for a man such as himself. His particular point had to do with selling drugs, but his larger message seemed to be that anything he did—

including robbing other blacks or mistreating black women—could be justified on the basis of what the white man had done to him.

While researching a previous book, *A Man's World,* I interviewed a highly educated black woman who recounted several unpleasant encounters she had had with black men. "Black men punish you for the ills of society. *They punish women,*" she insisted. Invited to speculate on why that might be, she talked at length of the particular pressures society places on black men, and she compared our plight with that of her white spouse: "My husband walks out of the door, and he knows the taxi is going to stop for him. It isn't a thing that he thinks about. . . . It's *their* world."

There is something to what she said. To be born a black male in America is to be put into shackles and then challenged to escape. Those shackles are as daunting as any faced by Houdini. But just as the handcuffs, the prisons cells, even the coffins that confined Houdini eventually bent to his will, the chains that bind us will yield as well, provided that we attack them shrewdly.

The trick (one of them, anyway) is to learn where to spend your energies and where not to. Griping about the state of society, therapeutic though that may be, has its limits as a life-improvement strategy. And justifying criminal acts or cruel behavior by pointing to what the white man has done becomes, at some point, nothing more than an exercise in moral irresponsibility—and a willful rejection of one's own capacity for change. Obviously, there is much that is wrong with a society that dumps people into ghettos and then blames them for being there; or that cannot figure out a way to adequately educate its young; or that sends millions to prisons, particularly when most of those imprisoned belong to so-called minority groups. The rising suicide rate, the growing prison population, the continuing academic achievement gap—all are particulars in a damning indictment of what America has done to some of her African-descended native sons.

But the cold fact is that life is hard for lots of people, and the fact that it may be harder for us is not likely, these days, to garner us much sympathy. Indeed, given the twisted logic that governs our so-called meritocracy, any troubles we are having at succeeding are taken as proof of our own unworthiness.

The good news is that today's America is not your grandfather's or even your father's America. We are no longer prohibited from going after what we deserve. We are no longer forced to hide our ambition while masking our bitterness with a grin. We can even dream of becoming heads of major corporations, cabinet secretaries, and big time crossover entrepreneurs. We don't face, as did our forefathers, a society committed to relentlessly humiliating us, to forcing us to play the role of inferiors in every civilized sphere. This doesn't mean that we are any closer today than we were in Fred Hampton's time to achieving the all-encompassing revolution, to reaching that lofty state of exalted consciousness that sweeps all inequities away. Nor does it mean that we are finally close to getting our forty acres and a mule. No one, it seems, is in much of a mood to give us anything, even though the right to reparations was earned with our ancestors' blood. What it does mean is that we have a certain social and cultural leeway; that, in a way our forefathers could only dream about, we are free to define our place in the world.

That freedom, for all the reasons we have previously explored, is nowhere near absolute. We still, in many respects, are at a decided disadvantage. But today's obstacles are not nearly as daunting as those faced by our ancestors. Call it the difference between stepping into the ring with both hands lashed behind your back and stepping in with one hand swinging free.

Still, if the one hand is all you have, you must use it twice as well as your opponent uses his. And because you have so much less room for error, you must fight strategically, understanding when to retreat and when to go all out and how to deflect the blows that inevitably will come your way. You must understand, in short, how to compete in this new arena, where the rules are neither what they seem nor quite what they used to be. So what I have set out below is a list of things that may help us in our competition. Call them new world rules, or keys to survival, or Cose's commandments; or, better yet, call them hard truths of this new age—an age of both unlimited potential and soul-crushing inequality.

Hard Truth 1: **Play the race card carefully, and at your own peril.** As Johnnie Cochran cleverly demonstrated as he saved O. J. Simpson's skin, there is a time when playing the race card makes perfectly good sense. In November 2000, researchers at the University of Michigan published a study showing that white mock jurors were especially likely to find blacks guilty in seemingly racially neutral situations. But when an explicit racial context was provided, their perceptions changed. The researchers used mixed race—black and white—couples for their experiment. In one scenario, the assailant, who was always of a different race than his girlfriend, shouted, "You know better than to talk that way about a man in front of his friends," before slapping her. In the other, before hitting the woman, the attacker screamed, "You know better than to talk that way about a white (or black) man in front of his friends." When race explicitly entered the equation, whites were no longer so likely to see blacks as more guilty; they treated black and white defendants more or less, equally. "When racial issues arise in a trial, white mock jurors are on guard against the possibility of prejudicial feelings and maintain the appearance of fairness. But when racial issues are not made explicit, white jurors are lenient toward the white defendant and more punitive toward the black defendant," observed investigator Samuel Sommers. (Blacks, by the way, generally were biased in favor of the black defendant, irrespective of the scenario.) The lesson seems to be that there is some value in certain circumstances in reminding people about the reality of racism; for when they are reminded of racisim (which is different from being accused of it), they make a greater attempt to be fair. Life, however, usually is not conducted under controlled experimental conditions. And as the Simpson trial demonstrated very clearly, Americans see racially charged incidents very differently, and much of that difference has to do with our dissimilar experiences with and perceptions of race. We (meaning blacks) have been so battered by and sensitized to racism that we sometimes see it where it doesn't exist. Whites have such an emotional investment in denying that they are racists that they often refuse to acknowledge racism when it is perfectly obvious to us. Other racial groups, depending on their experiences and sensitivities, also view racially-tinged incidents through an ethnocentric lens. Given such a psychologically complex phenomena as racial guilt and racial pain, you are not likely to find much empathy or understanding when you bring racial complaints to whites. The best you can generally hope for is an awkward silence accompanied by the suspicion that you are crying wolf. This is not to say that you should grin and bear bad treatment, but that you are generally better off finding a less charged terrain than that of racial grievance on which to fight the battle.

Hard Truth 2: **Complain all you like about the raw deal you have gotten in life, but don't expect those complaints to get you anywhere.** This is very much related to the preceding reality. America likes winners, not whiners. And one of the encouraging developments of this new, more enlightened age is that America even, at times, embraces winners who are black. There is a certain strong incentive to do so, since the very existence of black winners can be made into a rather fantastical argument that discrimination no longer hinders black advancement. Whiners, on the other hand, simply remind too many Americans of history they would prefer to forget, and of unpleasant current realities they would prefer not to face. The fact is that you almost inevitably will have it harder than a comparably placed white man, and you can expect racial bias (in either subtle or blatant form) to be a continuing factor in your life. But you can't be paralyzed because of that; nor, for the sake of your own sanity, can you afford to take it personally—or to expect much compassion in dealing with it. Thankfully, we have moved past the time when whites collectively spent much time hating us; these days they mostly just don't care. Did that boss (teacher, classmate, administrator, stranger) call you stupid because of your color, or despite it? Were you assumed to be a ballplayer instead of a scholar simply because you're black? Was your rival promoted ahead of you because he's white? Was your intellect (ability, judgment) questioned in an instance where your white colleague's would not have been? You can drive yourself crazy trying to figure it out and also end up wasting a lot of energy that could be best directed elsewhere. An editor in Chicago, where I began my writing career, gave me a valuable piece of advice. "If you're going to be a writer," he said, "you'd better develop a thick skin." Much the same could be said about just being a black man in America. If you are going to survive with your sanity and emotional health intact, you're going to have to learn not to sweat much of the routine stuff that makes being a black man difficult. If you can engage life with a certain amount of humor, or at least with a sense of charity, you'll not only be happier but a lot less likely to need blood pressure medication.

Hard Truth 3: **Expect to do better than the world expects of you; expect to live in a bigger world than the one you see.** One of the most unfortunate realities of growing up as a black male in America is that we are constantly told to lower our sights; we are constantly nudged, unless we are very lucky and privileged, in the direction of mediocrity. Our dreams, we are told in effect, cannot be as large as other folks' dreams; our universe, we are led to believe, will be smaller that of our nonblack peers. When Franklin Raines reminisced about "a period of time when my world grew bigger," he was describing the natural progression of knowledge and the optimal progression of life. When Arthur Ashe wrote that his "potential is more than can be expressed within the bounds of my race or ethnic identity," he was speaking for all of us. When Maurice Ashley talks of a "rope of destiny pulling me along," he is talking of something we all should feel. For those of us who are accustomed to hearing "You will never amount to much," dreams may be all that gives us the strength to go on. And as we dream big dreams, we also must prepare ourselves to pursue them, instead of contenting ourselves with fantasies of a wonderful existence that will be forever beyond our reach.

Hard Truth 4: **Don't expect support for your dreams from those who have not accomplished very much in their lives.** The natural reaction of many people (especially those who believe they share your background) is to feel threatened, intimidated, or simply to be dismissive if you are trying to do things they have not done themselves. When ex-prisoner Mike Gibson spoke of certain members of his own family putting him down for going to college, I was reminded of a piece of advice I read as a very young man. As a "junior leader" in my neighborhood Boys Club, I was invited to a dinner at which multimillionaire W. Clement Stone spoke. After delivering a stirring talk detailing his personal journey of success, Stone handed out an inspirational book (whose title I can no longer recall), which I took with me to bed that evening. Don't share your dreams with failures, warned the book, which went on to explain that people who had not done much in their own lives would be incapable of seeing the potential in yours. While that is certainly not true in all cases, it is true much too often. The book's observation helped me to understand why some people I knew seemed more interested in telling me what I could never accomplish than in helping me achieve what I could. It also helped me understand why I owed it to myself to tune out the voices around me telling me to lower my sights.

Hard Truth 5: **If someone is bringing out your most self-destructive tendencies, acknowledge that that person is not a friend.** No one should, willy-nilly, toss away friendship. People who will care for you, who will support and watch out for you, are a precious part of a full and blessed life. But people who claim to be friends are not always friends in fact. One of the lessons prison taught him, said Mike Gibson, was to "surround myself with people who want to see me do good." On the streets he learned that when things got tough, the very buddies who had encouraged him to break the law were nowhere to be found: "When I was in the cell, I was there by myself. . . . I always found myself alone." It's easy to be seduced by those who offer idiotic opinions disguised as guidance, by voices telling us, in effect, "Man enough to pull a gun, be man enough to squeeze it." It's even easier to find people who attach themselves to you for their own selfish reasons, or who will say they have your back when, in reality, they're only looking out for themselves. It's sometimes a bit harder to let them go, which sometimes is what you must do in the interest of your own survival.

Hard Truth 6: **Don't be too proud to ask for help, particularly from those who are wiser and older.** While working on

Color-Blind, I interviewed mathematician Philip Uri Triesman, who has had astounding success teaching advanced mathematics to black students who previously had not done very well. Unlike Chinese-American students who typically studied in groups, blacks, he had discovered, tended to study alone. For blacks, the solitary study ritual seemed to be a matter of pride, reflecting their need to prove that they could get by without help, that they were not inferior to whites. By getting them, in effect, to emulate some of what the Chinese Americans were doing, Triesman spurred the black students to unprecedented levels of accomplishment. Too often (and not only in math), we feel we have to face our problems alone. We feel (to repeat a phrase from Mike Gibson) as if we are the only ones "in the fuckin' world going through this shit everyday." We are uncomfortable admitting our pain, our inexperience, our incompetence; and, as a result, we sometimes ignore resources we usefully could tap. It is only now, looking back at my own life, that I am fully aware how fortunate I was that some exceptional people extended a hand. There were Gwendolyn Brooks, the poet laureate, and Ron Fair, the novelist, who recognized when I was merely a teenager that I had a writing talent worth encouraging; and there were the Chicago *Sun-Times* editors, James Hoge and Ralph Otwell, who allowed me, as an inexperienced eighteen-year-old would-be columnist, to talk my way into a writing job on the paper and, less than a year later, took a huge gamble by rewarding me with a weekly op-ed column in the full-run daily. Whether in schools, in the streets, or in corporate suites, too many of us are trying to cope alone when we would be much better off if we reached out for help.

Hard Truth 7: **Recognize that being true to yourself is not the same as being true to a stupid stereotype.** A few years ago when I visited Xavier University, a historically black college in New Orleans, I was moved by a student who proudly proclaimed the university to be a school full of nerds. At a time when many black men and boys are trying their best to act like mack-daddies and bad-ass muthafuckas, Xavier (which sends more blacks to medical schools than any other university) is saying that it has another image in mind: Blackness really has nothing to do with projecting a manufactured, crude street persona. Xavier celebrates accomplishment instead of denigrating it, and it makes no apologies for doing so. Useni Eugene Perkins, director of the Family Life Center at Chicago State University, talked poignantly of how it came to be that much of the black middle class was ashamed to acknowledge what it was; yet, he pointed out, much of the help for poor black communities would, of necessity, have to come from the middle class. "And I don't think you have to be apologetic about being middle class.... We shouldn't be arrogant or belligerent; but we can be role models." Fact is, we desperately need to promote archetypes other than rappers, thugs, and ballplayers of what it is possible and desirable for us to be—if for no other reason than so few of us can find success on such limited terrain.

Hard Truth 8: **Don't let the glitter blind you.** Almost invariably when I have spoken to people who had made their living selling drugs, they talk a lot like "Frank," who said, "I didn't want to be the only dude on the streets with busted-up shoes, old clothes." They talk of the money, the women, the cars, the gold chains—the glamour, the glitter, of the dealer's life. Only later do most acknowledge that the money, for most dealers, is not all that good, and that even when it is, it generally doesn't last very long—partly because the lifestyle so often leads to either prison or to an early grave. Maybe you don't care about that; maybe you see going to prison as a way of proving your manhood. Or maybe you believe you will be the big exception—that one in a million who actually has a long and prosperous life hustling. If so, I urge you to consider a few things:

1. You can count the numbers of us who have tried hustling and ended up in the penitentiary in the hundreds of thousands. You only need a couple of hands to count those, in black America, who have become long-term successful (by which, I mean wealthy) dealers. You have a better chance (provided you prepare for it) of getting a big job at a major corporation than of making big money for a long time on the streets—and the benefits and the security are a hell of a lot better.

2. If you have a child or even a younger brother, odds are your choices will influence theirs; so even if you're quite willing to risk your own future, or don't think you will live long anyway, or believe there is nothing better for you in this world, are you willing to condemn those whom you should care about to share your fate?

3. America has sold a lot of us a bogus bill of goods, convinced us that the only avenues available to us are hustling, selling dope, pimping, or engaging in other illegal acts that

generally land us in jail. If you have bought
that bill of goods, you owe it to yourself to
reconsider—because what that says is, at base,
you have very little confidence that you can do
anything other than fail. Face that fact, and
then discover that you are capable of more than
you believe.

Hard Truth 9: **Don't expect competence and hard work alone
to get you the recognition or rewards you deserve.** For all our
skepticism about the so-called system, it sometimes seems
that people of color are the only ones alive who truly believe
in the meritocracy. We work hard, pour all our energy into
our jobs, and then are stunned and shattered when our
hard work is not rewarded. Why, we ask, is our ability not
being recognized? Why is our hard work being overlooked?
Why can't they see our talent? The answers are as varied as
the possible circumstances, but the general rule is that any
organization (government, private business, educational,
or other) is essentially a social body that rewards those fully
engaged in the game. To the extent we try to hold ourselves
above that process, we end up losing.

Hard Truth 10: **You must seize the time, for it is already later
than you think.** When working on *The Rage of a Privileged
Class* I was touched by a confession from Basil Paterson,
lawyer, high-ranking Democratic National Committee
official, and former deputy mayor of New York. "Every day
I realize that I'm further ahead than I ever thought I would
be in my life. Yet . . . by any standard that is uniquely
American, I'm not successful. It's too late for me to get rich
because I spent too much time preparing for what I've

got. . . . Most of us are ten years behind what we should have been. We didn't get credentials until we were older than other folks," he said. Paterson was talking of a particular generation, one hobbled by a much more blatant, more virulent form of discrimination than exists for the most part today; but the essence of what he said is still true—at least for those not privileged enough to have well-to-do parents or fancy educations. As Daniel Rose tells his young disciples at the Harlem Educational Activities Fund, "Your chief competitor started yesterday. And you are already a day behind." While it is never too late to accomplish something in life, the longer you wait to get on track, the higher the odds that you will not reach your goals. Some years ago when running a program that trained minority journalists, I noticed that many of our young people entered the job market at a decided disadvantage to their white peers. Apparently no one had impressed upon them the fact that summer internships were the usual entry route to many major publications, so they had not made it a point to get any. Once lost, such ground is hard to make up, and it only gets harder, the longer one waits, as competition becomes even stiffer and opportunities dry up. Time can be over before you realize you have wasted it. Treat it like the precious commodity that it is.

*Hard Truth 11: **Even if you have to fake it, show some faith in yourself.*** Confidence, lightly worn, can be contagious, and you might even manage to fool yourself into letting go of your doubts. "A lot of our kids don't believe in themselves because they've been told by so many people that they ain't worth shit. I was labeled the bad kid, so I know how that feels," says youth worker J. W. Hughes. "Go to any high school with black males and tell them they are smart enough to go to any university in the world. Many of them will say, 'Not me.' I know that because [I was] one of them," says Omega Boys Club member Zachary Donald. So much energy has been expended undermining our confidence, picking apart our faith in ourselves, that we sometimes forget that faith does not depend on the beliefs of others or on demonstrating a list of accomplishments. "Faith is the substance of things hoped for, the evidence of things not seen," says the Bible (Hebrews 11:1). And there is so much that we have not yet seen, so much waiting to be revealed when it comes to our potential on this planet. But the first step is to believe that we can go where others say we can't.

*Hard Truth 12: **Don't force innocent others to bear the price of your pain.*** Sister Simone Ponnet, executive director of Abraham House, spoke feelingly of ex-convicts and prisoners who lamented growing up fatherless, or with abusive fathers, and then ended up treating their own children no better. Even some of us who haven't been locked down at times feel so much pain, so much anger, that we feel justified in taking out our frustrations on everyone around us. Threatened in so many realms, unable to control the forces enveloping us, we sometimes try too hard to exert control in the few areas we think we can: sometimes over women, sometimes over children, and sometimes over random souls unlucky enough to get in our way. It's as if we want to force them to share our misery. Resisting the temptation to turn loved ones into targets can sometimes be extremely difficult, but before giving in to temptation, we should remind ourselves that those who love us are the best hope we have to regain whatever humanity we have lost; that they, in other words, are our salvation.

All that I have said focuses on the personal, on what we, as individuals, can do to improve the quality of our lives. This is not to say that I believe the only problems we have in America are individual ones, or that we have no obligations to the larger society. Nothing could be further from the truth. There are huge and systemic problems that remain, that prevent America from being the best country that it can be. We continue, as a country, to leave our young people uneducated and, often, illiterate. We continue to stress incarceration where we should be stressing human reclamation. We continue to confound the dream of true equality by rejecting the investments in remediation and infrastructure needed to achieve it. We continue to permit society, on the basis of nothing more than prejudice, to label young black men as undesirable, as troublemakers, and we throw up our hands in exasperation when the self-fulfilling prophecy becomes fact. The list could go on, but those (to repeat a sentiment I have expressed before) are subjects for another day.

This volume is purposely less concerned with the systemic, with the grand social changes needed, than it is with the personal, with some things you might want to consider as you figure out how to live your life. And, as such, I would like to end on a hopeful note, by restating what I sincerely believe to be true: There is more leeway than there has ever been in history for you to become whatever you would be; for you to accomplish whatever you dream; for you to escape the prisons of stereotypes and caricatures that our forefathers could not avoid.

We are entitled to our big dreams, we deserve to see many of them come true, just as we deserve an America that is as welcoming to us as it is to a white kid from Cuba, Croatia, or Ireland. We deserve, in other words, the fairness we have always been promised, and the opportunity to compete free of the burdens we have always carried, burdens economic, emotional, and historical, burdens that still stand in the way of us receiving our due and of America achieving a true meritocracy.